EDITOR: Maryanne Blacker

FOOD EDITOR: Pamela Clark

■ ■ ■

ART DIRECTOR: Robbylee Phelan

ARTISTS: Karen Harborow, Gillian Bibb

■ ■ ■

ASSISTANT FOOD EDITOR: Louise Patniotis

ASSOCIATE FOOD EDITOR: Enid Morrison

SENIOR HOME ECONOMISTS:
Kathy McGarry, Sophia Young

HOME ECONOMISTS: Frances Abdallaoui, Angela
Bresnahan, Annette Brien, Karen Buckley, Caroline
Jones, Jean Low

EDITORIAL COORDINATOR: Elizabeth Hooper

KITCHEN ASSISTANT: Amy Wong

■ ■ ■

STYLISTS: Marie-Helene Clauzon, Carolyn Fienberg,
Jane Hann, Cherise Koch

PHOTOGRAPHERS: Kevin Brown, Robert Clark,
Robert Taylor, Jon Waddy

■ ■ ■

HOME LIBRARY STAFF:

ASSISTANT EDITOR: Bridget van Tinteren

EDITORIAL COORDINATOR: Fiona Lambrou

■ ■ ■

ACP PUBLISHER: Richard Walsh

ACP DEPUTY PUBLISHER: Nick Chan

ACP CIRCULATION & MARKETING DIRECTOR:
Judy Kiernan

■ ■ ■

Produced by The Australian Women's Weekly Home Library.
Typeset by ACP Colour Graphics Pty Ltd.
Colour separations by Network Graphics Pty. Ltd. in Sydney.
Printing by Hannanprint in Sydney.
Published by ACP Publishing Pty Ltd, 54 Park Street, Sydney.
♦ **AUSTRALIA:** Distributed by Network Distribution Company,
54 Park Street Sydney, (02) 282 8777.
♦ **UNITED KINGDOM:** Distributed in the U.K. by Australian
Consolidated Press (UK) Ltd, 20 Galowhill Rd, Brackmills,
Northampton NN4 7EE (01604) 760 456.
♦ **CANADA:** Distributed in Canada by Whitecap Books Ltd,
351 Lynn Ave, North Vancouver B.C. V7J 2C4 (604) 980 9852.
♦ **NEW ZEALAND:** Distributed in New Zealand by Netlink
Distribution Company, 17B Hargreaves St, Level 5,
College Hill, Auckland 1 (9) 302 7616.
♦ **SOUTH AFRICA:** Distributed in South Africa by Intermag,
PO Box 57394, Springfield 2137 (011) 493 3200.

■ ■ ■

Rice Cookbook

Includes index.
ISBN 1 86396 033 3

1. Cookery (Rice). 2. Rice. I. Title:
Australian Women's Weekly. (Series:
Australian Women's Weekly Home Library).

641.6318

■ ■ ■

COVER: Clockwise from top left: Nutty Olive and Rice
Meatloaf, page 75; Chicken and Seafood Paella, page 33;
Spicy Prawn and Chicken Patties, page 64; Jasmine Rice Salad
with Chilli Coconut Dressing, page 90.
*China from Villeroy & Boch at Grace Bros; green bowl from The
Bay Tree Kitchen Shop; tiles from Country Floors.*
BACK COVER: From back, Mocha Risotto, Mexican-Style
Rice Pudding, page 106.

Rice
COOKBOOK

*Every grain of rice is a brilliant little package of
health and energy. Current research suggests
that the starch in cooked rice is extremely
important to our well-being — a bonus with
every one of our delicious recipes. There's an
international touch throughout, and the lovely
desserts will delight you. First, though, read our
helpful guide to rice on page 120.*

Pamela Clark

FOOD EDITOR

2 SNACKS, SOUPS &
LUNCHES
. . . .

28 MAIN COURSES
. . . .

80 ACCOMPANIMENTS
. . . .

100 DESSERTS
. . . .

120 RICE FOR HEALTH &
ENERGY
. . . .

121 GLOSSARY
. . . .

125 INDEX

BRITISH & NORTH AMERICAN READERS: Please note that
Australian cup and spoon measurements are metric. A quick
conversion guide appears on page 127.
A glossary explaining unfamiliar terms and ingredients appears on page 121.

Snacks, Soups & Lunches

From now on, you will think of rice as far more than an ordinary kitchen staple. Instead, you'll be delighted with its extraordinary versatility — it's the basis of our fabulous variety of tasty, tempting recipes, starting here with snacks, soups, light meals and lunches to please everyone; some would also be perfect entrees. For helpful rice cooking tips, turn to page 120.

THAI-STYLE FRIED RICE

1 tablespoon peanut oil
2 cloves garlic, crushed
1 teaspoon grated fresh ginger
2 teaspoons chopped fresh
   lemon grass
250g minced pork
1 stick celery, sliced
1 large (350g) red pepper, chopped
1 medium (120g) carrot, chopped
6 green shallots, chopped
1 cup (125g) frozen peas
2 cups cooked jasmine rice
440g can pineapple pieces in natural
   juice, drained
2 tablespoons chopped fresh basil
2 teaspoons brown sugar
¼ cup (60ml) lime juice
1 tablespoon soy sauce
1 teaspoon fish sauce
¼ cup chopped fresh coriander
¼ cup (35g) unsalted roasted
   peanuts, chopped

Heat oil in wok or pan, add garlic, ginger, lemon grass and pork, cook, stirring, until pork is browned. Add celery, pepper, carrot, shallots and peas, cook, stirring, until vegetables are tender. Add rice, pineapple, basil, sugar, juice and sauces, cook, stirring, until heated through. Serve sprinkled with coriander and peanuts.

Serves 4 to 6.

■ Rice is best cooked a day ahead.
■ Storage: Uncovered, in refrigerator.
■ Freeze: Cooked rice suitable.
■ Microwave: Suitable.

RIGHT: Thai-Style Fried Rice.

*China from Villeroy & Boch;
tiles from Country Floors.*

NUTTY CHEESE AND RICE FRITTATA

1 tablespoon light olive oil
2 bacon rashers, chopped
1 medium (150g) onion, sliced
2 medium (240g) zucchini, sliced
1 clove garlic, crushed
½ teaspoon chopped fresh rosemary
6 eggs, lightly beaten
1 cup cooked white short-grain rice
½ cup (60g) grated smoked cheese
¼ cup (40g) pine nuts

Heat oil in 25cm round non-stick shallow pan, add bacon, cook, stirring, until bacon is crisp. Add onion, zucchini, garlic and rosemary, cook, stirring, until onion is soft. Remove from heat, stir in eggs, rice and cheese; cook, covered, over low heat about 10 minutes or until mixture is almost set. Sprinkle with nuts, place under hot grill until browned and set.

Serves 4 to 6.

- Recipe can be prepared a day ahead.
- Storage: Covered, in refrigerator.
- Freeze: Cooked rice suitable.
- Microwave: Rice suitable.

BELOW: From back: Pepper and Prosciutto Rice Cake, Nutty Cheese and Rice Frittata.

Tiles from Country Floors.

PEPPER AND PROSCIUTTO RICE CAKE

1 large (500g) eggplant
coarse cooking salt
2 tablespoons olive oil
1 large (350g) red pepper
1 large (350g) yellow pepper
8 (120g) slices prosciutto
2 cups cooked white short-grain rice
½ cup cooked wild rice

CURRY SAUCE
70g butter
½ cup (75g) plain flour
2 teaspoons mild curry powder
1 teaspoon sugar
1½ cups (375ml) buttermilk
300ml cream
1 tablespoon chopped fresh parsley
2 tablespoons grated parmesan cheese

TOPPING
¼ cup (20g) grated parmesan cheese
1 tablespoon chopped fresh parsley
½ cup (35g) stale breadcrumbs
½ cup (40g) flaked almonds
20g butter, melted

Grease 22cm springform tin, cover base with foil. Cut eggplant into 5mm slices. Place slices on wire rack, sprinkle with salt, stand 30 minutes.

Rinse slices under cold water, drain on absorbent paper. Brush slices with about half the oil, place in single layer on oven trays, grill until lightly browned on both sides.

Quarter peppers, remove seeds and membranes. Grill peppers, skin side up, until skin blisters and blackens. Peel away skin, slice peppers. Heat remaining oil in pan, add prosciutto in batches, cook until crisp; drain on absorbent paper.

Combine all the rice and 2 cups (500ml) of the curry sauce in bowl. Spread one-third of the rice mixture over base of prepared tin, top with half the eggplant, then another third of the rice mixture, peppers, remaining rice mixture and remaining eggplant. Spread with remaining curry sauce, top with prosciutto, sprinkle with topping. Bake, uncovered, in moderate oven about 40 minutes or until browned.

Curry Sauce: Melt butter in pan, add flour, curry powder and sugar, cook, stirring, until dry and grainy. Remove from heat, gradually stir in buttermilk and cream, stir over heat until sauce boils and thickens, stir in parsley and cheese.

Topping: Combine all ingredients in bowl; mix well.

Serves 6.

- Recipe can be prepared a day ahead.
- Storage: Covered, in refrigerator.
- Freeze: Cooked rice suitable.
- Microwave: Rice and curry sauce suitable.

CORN AND CORIANDER SOUP

60g butter
1 medium (350g) leek, sliced
1 medium (120g) carrot,
finely chopped
1 clove garlic, crushed
1 teaspoon ground cumin
1 tablespoon plain flour
⅓ cup (65g) white short-grain rice
1 small (150g) green pepper,
finely chopped
1 small (150g) red pepper,
finely chopped
1.5 litres (6 cups) chicken stock
1 small fresh red chilli, finely chopped
310g can corn kernels, drained
2 tablespoons chopped fresh
coriander

Heat butter in pan, add leek, carrot, garlic
and cumin, cook, covered, 10 minutes,
or until leek is soft, stirring occasionally. Stir
in flour and rice, cook, stirring, 1 minute.
Add peppers, stock and chilli, simmer,
uncovered, about 20 minutes or until rice
is tender. Stir in corn and coriander.

Serves 4 to 6.

- Recipe can be made a day ahead.
- Storage: Covered, in refrigerator.
- Freeze: Suitable.
- Microwave: Not suitable.

MULLIGATAWNY SOUP

30g butter
1 small (200g) leek, sliced
1 stick celery, finely chopped
1 medium (120g) carrot,
finely chopped
2 tablespoons Madras curry paste
2 cloves garlic, crushed
2 teaspoons grated fresh ginger
½ cup (100g) white short-grain rice
1½ cups (375ml) coconut milk
1 medium (150g) apple, grated
2 tablespoons lime juice
2 tablespoons chopped fresh
coriander

CHICKEN STOCK
1.2kg chicken
5 litres (20 cups) water
15 black peppercorns
1 large (200g) onion, quartered
1 large (180g) carrot, chopped
1 stick celery, chopped
4 sprigs fresh parsley
2 bay leaves

Heat butter in large pan, add leek, celery,
carrot and paste, cook, stirring, until leek
is soft. Add garlic, ginger and rice, cook,
stirring, 3 minutes or until fragrant. Add
chicken stock, simmer, uncovered, 10
minutes. Add coconut milk, apple and
chopped chicken (from stock), simmer
5 minutes. Just before serving, stir in juice
and coriander.
Chicken Stock: Combine all ingredients
in large stock pot, simmer, uncovered,
1½ hours. Remove chicken, strain stock

into bowl, discard vegetable mixture.
Return chicken to stock; cool. Cover,
refrigerate several hours or overnight.

Next day, skim fat from stock, remove
chicken from stock, remove meat from
chicken, discard skin and bones; chop
chicken meat. You will need 2.5 litres
(10 cups) stock for this recipe. Freeze any
remaining stock for another use.

Serves 6 to 8.

- Recipe can be prepared a day ahead.
- Storage: Covered, in refrigerator.
- Freeze: Suitable.
- Microwave: Suitable.

*ABOVE: From left: Mulligatawny Soup,
Corn and Coriander Soup.*

*Wicker tray from Home & Garden on the Mall;
fabric from Les Olivades.*

SMOKED CHICKEN AND RICE SALAD

1 (250g) skinless smoked chicken
    breast, chopped
250g packet cream cheese, softened
1½ cups cooked brown rice and
    wild rice blend
1 tablespoon chopped fresh chives
¾ cup chopped fresh parsley
1 medium green oak leaf lettuce
1 small radicchio lettuce
200g smoked cheese, sliced

DRESSING
¼ cup (60ml) vegetable oil
2 tablespoons white wine vinegar
2 teaspoons Dijon mustard
1 teaspoon chopped fresh thyme
1 teaspoon sugar

Process chopped chicken, cream cheese
and ½ cup of the rice until smooth, stir in
chives. Roll rounded teaspoons of mixture into balls, toss in parsley; place on
tray, refrigerate until firm. Place lettuce
leaves, smoked cheese, remaining rice
and chicken balls on serving plate. Drizzle
with dressing just before serving.
Dressing: Combine all ingredients in
bowl; mix well.

Serves 4 to 6.

- Chicken balls can be made
  a day ahead.
- Storage: Covered, in refrigerator.
- Freeze: Cooked rice suitable.
- Microwave: Rice suitable.

CREAMY CHICKEN SOUP WITH CHEESY RICE BALLS

1.2kg chicken
4 litres (16 cups) water
1 medium (350g) leek, sliced
1 medium (120g) carrot, chopped
1 sprig fresh thyme
3 bacon rashers, sliced
1 medium (350g) leek, sliced, extra
200g broccoli, chopped
½ cup (125ml) cream
1 tablespoon chopped fresh chives
1 teaspoon chopped fresh thyme
1 tablespoon chicken stock powder

CHEESY RICE BALLS
2 cups cooked white long-grain rice
½ cup (40g) grated parmesan cheese
2 egg yolks

Combine chicken, water, leek, carrot and
thyme in large pan, bring to boil, simmer,
uncovered, 2 hours.

Remove chicken from pan, strain stock;
reserve 2 litres (8 cups) stock. Remove
skin from chicken, chop chicken; discard
skin and bones; return chicken to
reserved stock. Cool stock, cover,
refrigerate overnight.

Skim fat from stock. Combine bacon
and extra leek in large pan, cook, stirring,
until leek is soft. Stir in stock mixture
and remaining ingredients, simmer,
uncovered, until broccoli is just tender. Stir
in cheesy rice balls just before serving.
Cheesy Rice Balls: Process all ingredients until combined. Roll rounded
teaspoons of mixture into balls, using
damp hands.

Serves 4 to 6.

- Stock must be made a day ahead.
- Storage: Covered, in refrigerator.
- Freeze: Stock, soup and cooked
  rice suitable.
- Microwave: Rice suitable.

SPICY MINESTRONE SOUP WITH RICE CROUTONS

1 cup (200g) dried borlotti beans
1 tablespoon olive oil
1 medium (350g) leek, sliced
3 medium (360g) carrots,
    finely chopped
1 clove garlic, crushed
1 small fresh red chilli, chopped
½ cup (100g) white short-grain rice
2 litres (8 cups) beef stock
425g can tomatoes
100g pepperoni, thinly sliced
200g green beans, sliced
3 medium (360g) zucchini,
    finely chopped
1 tablespoon chopped fresh basil
1 tablespoon chopped fresh parsley

RICE CROUTONS
2 (24g) rice cakes
30g butter, melted
1 tablespoon olive oil
1 clove garlic, crushed
1 tablespoon chopped fresh basil

Place borlotti beans in bowl, cover well
with cold water, cover, stand overnight.

Drain borlotti beans. Heat oil in pan,
add leek, carrots, garlic and chilli, cook,
stirring, until leek is soft. Add borlotti
beans, rice, stock, undrained crushed
tomatoes and pepperoni, simmer,

uncovered, about 20 minutes, stirring occasionally. Stir in green beans and zucchini, simmer, uncovered, about 10 minutes or until vegetables are tender; stir in herbs. Serve with rice croutons.

Rice Croutons: Cut rice cakes into 1cm cubes. Combine with remaining ingredients in bowl; mix well. Heat non-stick pan, add rice mixture, cook, stirring, until browned. Drain on absorbent paper; cool.

Serves 6 to 8.

- Soup and croutons can be made a day ahead.
- Storage: Soup, covered, in refrigerator. Croutons, in airtight container.
- Freeze: Soup suitable.
- Microwave: Soup suitable.

PESTO, RICE AND VEGETABLE SOUP

2 fresh corn cobs
1 tablespoon olive oil
2 medium (700g) leeks, sliced
1 bunch (430g) baby carrots, sliced
1 large (350g) red pepper, finely chopped
2 teaspoons chopped fresh thyme
2 litres (8 cups) water
3 teaspoons vegetable stock powder
2 medium (240g) zucchini, chopped
1 cup cooked brown rice

PESTO
1 cup firmly packed fresh basil leaves
1/2 cup (40g) grated parmesan cheese
2 cloves garlic, crushed
2 tablespoons walnuts, toasted
1 tablespoon olive oil
1/4 cup (60ml) water

Cut kernels from corn cobs. Heat oil in large pan, add leeks, carrots, pepper and thyme, cook, stirring, for 5 minutes. Add water and stock powder to pan, bring to boil, simmer, uncovered, 5 minutes. Skim soup, if necessary. Add zucchini, corn and rice to soup, cook about 5 minutes or until vegetables are just tender. Stir in pesto just before serving.

Pesto: Process all the ingredients until combined.

Serves 4 to 6.

- Recipe can be made a day ahead.
- Storage: Covered, in refrigerator.
- Freeze: Suitable.
- Microwave: Soup suitable.

LEFT: Smoked Chicken and Rice Salad.
ABOVE: Clockwise from top left: Creamy Chicken Soup with Cheesy Rice Balls, Spicy Minestrone Soup with Rice Croutons, Pesto, Rice and Vegetable Soup.

Above: Bowls from House.

HASHBROWNS WITH ONION TOMATO RELISH

2 medium (400g) potatoes, coarsely grated
1 tablespoon olive oil
1 clove garlic, crushed
3 green shallots, chopped
130g can corn kernels, drained
¾ cup cooked white long-grain rice
1 tablespoon chopped fresh coriander
2 tablespoons plain flour
1 egg, lightly beaten
vegetable oil for shallow-frying

ONION TOMATO RELISH
2 teaspoons olive oil
20g butter
1 medium (150g) onion, sliced
3 medium (225g) egg tomatoes, chopped
1 tablespoon balsamic vinegar
1 teaspoon sugar
2 tablespoons chopped fresh parsley

Squeeze excess moisture from potatoes. Heat olive oil in pan, add garlic, shallots and corn, cook, stirring, about 5 minutes. Remove from heat, stir in potatoes, rice, coriander, flour and egg; mix well.

Heat vegetable oil in pan for shallow-frying, add ¼ cup of mixture, flatten slightly. Shallow-fry slowly until browned on both sides; drain on absorbent paper. Repeat with remaining mixture. Serve hashbrowns with onion tomato relish.

Onion Tomato Relish: Heat oil and butter in pan, add onion, cook, stirring, over low heat about 15 minutes or until onion is soft and golden brown. Stir in remaining ingredients.

Serves 6 to 8.

- Recipe best made close to serving.
- Freeze: Cooked rice suitable.
- Microwave: Rice suitable.

SPICY PATTIES WITH CORIANDER CREAM SAUCE

1 tablespoon olive oil
1 medium (150g) onion, finely chopped
1 large (350g) red pepper, finely chopped
1 clove garlic, crushed
1 medium (120g) zucchini, grated
100g csabai sausage, finely chopped
⅓ cup (25g) grated parmesan cheese
1 tablespoon chopped fresh parsley
1½ cups cooked white short-grain rice
1 egg, lightly beaten
1 cup (70g) stale breadcrumbs
plain flour
vegetable oil for shallow-frying

CORIANDER CREAM SAUCE
1 cup (250ml) sour light cream
2 teaspoons seeded mustard
1 clove garlic, crushed
1 tablespoon tomato paste
1 tablespoon chopped fresh coriander

Heat olive oil in pan, add onion, pepper, garlic, zucchini and sausage, cook, stirring, until vegetables are soft. Transfer mixture to bowl, add cheese, parsley, rice, egg and breadcrumbs; mix well. Shape mixture into 8 patties, using damp hands; refrigerate patties 2 hours.

Toss patties in flour, shake away excess flour. Heat vegetable oil in pan, shallow-fry patties until browned and cooked through. Serve with coriander cream sauce.

Coriander Cream Sauce: Combine all ingredients in bowl: mix well.

Serves 4.

- Recipe can be prepared a day ahead.
- Storage: Covered, separately, in refrigerator.
- Freeze: Cooked rice suitable.
- Microwave: Rice suitable.

LEFT: From back: Spicy Patties with Coriander Cream Sauce, Hashbrowns with Onion Tomato Relish.

China by Johnson Brothers for Waterford Wedgwood; basket and glasses from House.

SALAMI RICE PANCAKES WITH RED PEPPER SAUCE

1 cup (150g) self-raising flour
1 cup cooked white long-grain rice
30g butter, melted
1 egg, lightly beaten
¾ cup (180ml) milk
150g mild salami, sliced

PESTO
1 cup firmly packed fresh
**   basil leaves**
1 clove garlic, crushed
1 tablespoon pine nuts, toasted
¼ cup (60ml) olive oil
⅓ cup (80ml) light sour cream

RED PEPPER SAUCE
1 large (350g) red pepper, chopped
1 tablespoon balsamic vinegar
1 tablespoon lemon juice
2 tablespoons olive oil

Sift flour into bowl, stir in rice, butter, egg and milk; stir until combined. Add ¼ cup of mixture to heated, greased heavy-based pan, cook until browned on both sides. You will need 8 pancakes.

Add salami to dry pan, cook, stirring, until crisp; drain on absorbent paper. Serve warm pancakes with salami, pesto and red pepper sauce.

Pesto: Blend or process basil, garlic, nuts and oil until combined. Transfer pesto to bowl, whisk in sour cream. Press plastic wrap onto surface of pesto mixture; refrigerate until firm.

Red Pepper Sauce: Blend all ingredients until combined.

Serves 4.

- ▪ Pesto and red pepper sauce can be made a day ahead.
- ▪ Storage: Covered, separately, in refrigerator.
- ▪ Freeze: Cooked rice suitable.
- ▪ Microwave: Rice suitable.

EGGPLANT BACON ROLLS

1 large (500g) eggplant
coarse cooking salt
vegetable oil for shallow-frying
2 bacon rashers, finely chopped
1 cup cooked white short-grain rice
⅓ cup (25g) grated parmesan cheese
2 tablespoons drained chopped
**   sun-dried tomatoes**
¼ cup chopped fresh parsley
½ cup (35g) stale breadcrumbs
1 egg yolk

Cut eggplant lengthways into 7mm slices; you will need 8 slices for this recipe. Place slices on wire rack, sprinkle with salt, stand 30 minutes. Rinse slices under cold water, drain on absorbent paper. Shallow-fry slices in hot oil until browned on both sides; drain well on absorbent paper.

Cook bacon in pan, stirring, until browned and crisp; drain on absorbent paper. Combine bacon with remaining ingredients in bowl; mix well. Divide mixture into 8 portions, place a portion on shortest end of each eggplant slice. Roll up and place on oven tray, bake, uncovered, in moderate oven about 15 minutes or until hot. Drain on absorbent paper.

Serves 4.

- ▪ Recipe can be prepared a day ahead.
- ▪ Storage: Covered, in refrigerator.
- ▪ Freeze: Cooked rice suitable.
- ▪ Microwave: Rice suitable.

ABOVE: From back: Eggplant Bacon Rolls, Salami Rice Pancakes with Red Pepper Sauce.

STICKY RICE ROLLS

½ cup (100g) black glutinous rice
1 tablespoon olive oil
1 small (200g) leek, finely chopped
150g mushrooms, finely chopped
1 clove garlic, crushed
310g can corn kernels, drained
1¼ cups (250g) finely chopped
  cooked chicken
2 tablespoons chopped fresh parsley
¼ cup (40g) pine nuts, toasted
10 x 25cm square spring roll
  wrappers
1 egg yolk
1 tablespoon water
vegetable oil for deep-frying

CHILLI SAUCE
¾ cup (180ml) chicken stock
½ cup (125ml) mild sweet chilli sauce
1 tablespoon honey

Place rice in bowl, cover well with cold water, cover; stand overnight.

Drain rice, add to large pan of boiling water, boil, uncovered, until tender; drain, rinse well. Heat olive oil in pan, add leek, mushrooms and garlic, cook, stirring, until leek is soft. Add corn, cook, stirring, until any liquid has evaporated. Transfer mixture to medium bowl. Add chicken, parsley, nuts and rice; mix well.

Brush edges of spring roll wrappers lightly with combined egg yolk and water. Place ⅓ cup of the mixture evenly across 1 corner of each wrapper, roll wrapper, tucking in ends. Deep-fry rolls in hot vegetable oil until golden brown; drain on absorbent paper. Serve with chilli sauce.

Chilli Sauce: Combine all ingredients in small pan, simmer, uncovered, 10 minutes or until slightly thickened.

Serves 4 to 6.

■ Recipe can be made 2 days ahead.
■ Storage: Covered, separately, in refrigerator.
■ Freeze: Uncooked rolls suitable.
■ Microwave: Not suitable.

ABOVE: Sticky Rice Rolls.

Plate from Plumes Gift Agencies; tray and utensils from Morris Home & Garden Wares.

ROAST PORK STIR-FRY IN RICE BASKETS

1 tablespoon peanut oil
1 clove garlic, crushed
1 teaspoon grated fresh ginger
1 large (200g) onion, sliced
1 large (350g) red pepper, sliced
200g piece Chinese roast pork, sliced
1 bunch (500g) baby bok choy, chopped
¼ teaspoon five spice powder
1 tablespoon oyster sauce
1 tablespoon water

RICE BASKETS
½ cup (75g) brown rice flour
1 cup cooked jasmine rice
3 eggs, lightly beaten
½ teaspoon Szechuan pepper
1 teaspoon sesame oil
⅓ cup (80ml) milk

Add oil to heated wok or pan, add garlic, ginger, onion and pepper, stir-fry until onion is soft. Add remaining ingredients, stir-fry until bok choy is just wilted. Serve in rice baskets.

Rice Baskets: Sift flour into bowl, stir in remaining ingredients. Spoon ⅓ cup mixture into heated greased pan, quickly spread to 17cm round; cook over low heat until just set underneath, turn over, cook until just set on other side. Repeat with remaining mixture. You will need 4 rice rounds for this recipe.

Shape each warm rice round over an upturned metal dish (1 cup capacity) to make baskets, place on oven tray. Bake in moderately hot oven about 20 minutes or until crisp.

Serves 4.

■ Recipe best made just before serving.
■ Freeze: Cooked rice suitable.
■ Microwave: Rice suitable.

BELOW: Roast Pork Stir-Fry in Rice Baskets.

RICE AND CHEESE TORTE

2 tablespoons polenta
4 cups (800g) ricotta cheese
1 cup (125g) grated tasty cheddar
   cheese
⅓ cup (25g) grated parmesan cheese
1 cup cooked white long-grain rice
3 eggs, separated
1 tablespoon chopped fresh
   rosemary
1 tablespoon chopped fresh sage
2 tablespoons grated parmesan
   cheese, extra

Grease 22cm springform tin, cover base with foil, grease foil. Sprinkle base and side of prepared tin with polenta. Combine ricotta, cheddar and parmesan cheeses with rice, egg yolks and herbs in large bowl; mix well. Beat egg whites in small bowl with electric mixer until firm peaks form, fold into the cheese mixture in 2 batches. Pour mixture into prepared tin, sprinkle with extra cheese. Bake, uncovered, in moderately hot oven about 1 hour or until firm.

Serves 6 to 8.

- Recipe can be made a day ahead.
- Storage: Covered, in refrigerator.
- Freeze: Cooked rice suitable.
- Microwave: Rice suitable.

GRILLED VEGETABLE FLAN

2 cups cooked brown rice
1 egg, lightly beaten
½ cup (40g) grated parmesan cheese
2 medium (400g) red peppers
4 medium (480g) zucchini
1 tablespoon olive oil
2 tablespoons bottled pesto
2 eggs, lightly beaten, extra
½ cup (125ml) cream

Process half the rice until finely chopped. Combine processed rice, remaining rice, egg and cheese in bowl; mix well. Press rice mixture over base and side of greased 23cm shallow pie dish.

Quarter peppers, remove seeds and membranes. Grill peppers, skin side up, until skin blisters and blackens. Peel away skin, cut peppers into 3cm strips. Cut zucchini lengthways into 7mm slices, brush with oil, grill until browned on both sides. Spread pesto over rice base, top with peppers and zucchini. Pour combined extra eggs and cream over vegetables. Bake, uncovered, in moderate oven about 35 minutes or until set.

Serves 4 to 6.

- Recipe can be made a day ahead.
- Storage: Covered, in refrigerator.
- Freeze: Cooked rice suitable.
- Microwave: Rice suitable.

MULTIGRAIN BREAD

2 teaspoons (7g) dried yeast
2 tablespoons brown sugar
1¾ cups (430ml) warm water
3¼ cups (520g) wholemeal plain flour
2 tablespoons gluten flour
½ cup (75g) rye flour
⅓ cup (50g) brown rice flour
1½ teaspoons salt
½ cup cooked brown rice
½ cup cooked pearl barley
⅓ cup (30g) rolled oats
¼ cup (60ml) vegetable oil
2 tablespoons rolled oats, extra

Grease 15cm x 25cm loaf pan. Combine yeast and sugar in small bowl, stir in ½ cup (125ml) of the warm water, stand in warm place about 10 minutes or until mixture is frothy.

Sift flours and salt into large bowl, stir in rice, barley and oats; make well in centre. Stir in yeast mixture, oil and remaining water, mix to a firm dough. Knead dough on floured surface about 10 minutes or until dough is smooth and elastic. Place dough in oiled bowl, cover; stand in warm place about 30 minutes or until dough is almost doubled in size.

Turn dough onto floured surface, knead until smooth. Shape dough into a loaf, place in prepared pan, cover; stand in warm place about 30 minutes or until dough reaches just over the top of the pan. Brush top of loaf with water, sprinkle with extra oats. Bake in moderately hot oven 30 minutes, reduce heat to moderate, bake further 30 minutes or until loaf sounds hollow when tapped. Turn onto wire rack to cool.

- Recipe best made on day of serving.
- Storage: Airtight container.
- Freeze: Suitable.
- Microwave: Rice and barley suitable.

LEFT: From back: Rice and Cheese Torte, Grilled Vegetable Flan.

Tiles from Country Floors.

SUSHI

6 cups hot cooked white
short-grain rice
⅓ cup (80ml) rice vinegar
¼ cup (55g) sugar
1 teaspoon salt
1 small (130g) green cucumber
1 small (200g) avocado
2 eggs, lightly beaten
2 teaspoons water
1 teaspoon soy sauce
5 sheets roasted nori
1 tablespoon preserved ginger

WASABI MAYONNAISE
½ cup (125ml) mayonnaise
1½ teaspoons wasabi paste
½ teaspoon soy sauce

Place hot rice in large non-metallic bowl, gradually add combined vinegar, sugar and salt as you toss rice with a spatula. At the same time, you will need someone to fan the rice so that it cools rapidly and becomes very glossy.

Cut cucumber in half lengthways, reserve 1 half for another use. Remove seeds from cucumber, cut cucumber into long, thin strips. Peel avocado, cut into thin strips.

Combine eggs, water and soy sauce in another bowl. Heat 22cm non-stick pan, pour in egg mixture, cook, without stirring, until set. Remove omelette from pan, roll up firmly; cut into 1cm strips.

Place 1 sheet of nori, rough side up, on damp bamboo sushi mat. Dip fingers in water and spread a fifth of the rice over nori, pressing down firmly, leaving 4cm strip on far side. Place some cucumber, avocado, egg strips and ginger across centre of rice.

Starting at the edge closest to you, use bamboo mat to help roll the sushi, pressing firmly as you roll. Remove bamboo mat, use a sharp knife to trim ends, cut sushi into 6 pieces. Serve with wasabi mayonnaise.

Wasabi Mayonnaise: Combine all ingredients in bowl; mix well.

Makes 30.

- Recipe can be made several hours ahead.
- Storage: Covered, in refrigerator.
- Freeze: Rice suitable.
- Microwave: Rice suitable.

LEFT: Multigrain Bread.
ABOVE: Sushi.

WONTON SOUP

1 medium (120g) carrot, thinly sliced
1 litre (4 cups) water
2 cups (500ml) beef stock
2 teaspoons grated fresh ginger
3 teaspoons soy sauce
3 green shallots, chopped
250g flat rice noodles
1 tablespoon fresh coriander leaves

WONTONS
2 Chinese dried mushrooms
1 teaspoon peanut oil
1 clove garlic, chopped
1 small (80g) onion, finely chopped
1 teaspoon sesame oil
200g pork and veal mince
2 teaspoons soy sauce
½ teaspoon sambal oelek
2 tablespoons chopped water
    chestnuts
30 x 8cm square egg pastry
    wonton wrappers

Combine carrot, water, stock, ginger, sauce and shallots in large pan, simmer, covered, about 5 minutes or until carrot is tender. Add noodles and wontons, simmer, uncovered, about 5 minutes or until wontons float to the surface and are cooked through. Stir in coriander.

Wontons: Place mushrooms in heatproof bowl, cover with boiling water, stand 20 minutes. Drain mushrooms; discard stems, chop caps. Heat peanut oil in pan, add garlic and onion, cook, stirring, until onion is soft. Combine onion mixture, mushrooms, sesame oil, pork and veal, sauce, sambal oelek and water chestnuts in bowl; mix well. Place rounded teaspoons of mixture in centre of each wonton wrapper, brush edges lightly with water. Pull up edges of pastry around mixture, pinch together to seal.

Serves 6.

■ Wontons can be prepared a day ahead. Soup base can be made a day ahead.
■ Storage: Covered, separately, in refrigerator.
■ Freeze: Uncooked wontons suitable.
■ Microwave: Soup base suitable.

BELOW: Wonton Soup.

RICE AND BARLEY COUNTRY SOUP

1 tablespoon olive oil
2 cloves garlic, crushed
2 medium (700g) leeks, chopped
2 slices (30g) pancetta, chopped
**7 medium (525g) egg tomatoes,
     peeled, seeded, chopped**
1 large (300g) potato, chopped
½ cup (100g) brown rice
⅓ cup (65g) pearl barley
2 litres (8 cups) chicken stock
2 teaspoons chopped fresh sage
3 medium (360g) zucchini, chopped
**2 tablespoons parmesan
     cheese flakes**
1 tablespoon shredded fresh basil

Heat oil in large pan, add garlic, leeks and pancetta, cook, stirring, until leeks are soft. Add tomatoes, potato, rice, barley and stock, simmer, covered, about 35 minutes or until rice and barley are tender. Stir in sage and zucchini, simmer, uncovered, further 5 minutes or until zucchini is tender. Serve topped with cheese and basil.

Serves 6.

■ Recipe best made just before serving.
■ Freeze: Not suitable.
■ Microwave: Suitable.

HAM AND ZUCCHINI MUFFINS

2 cups (300g) self-raising flour
1 cup cooked white long-grain rice
100g ham, finely chopped
¾ cup (60g) grated parmesan cheese
**2 small (180g) zucchini, coarsely
     grated**
2 eggs, lightly beaten
1 cup (250ml) milk
90g butter, melted
1 tablespoon seeded mustard

Grease 12 hole muffin pan (⅓ cup/80ml capacity). Combine all ingredients in large bowl, stir with metal spoon until just combined. Spoon mixture into prepared pan. Bake in moderately hot oven about 25 minutes or until muffins are browned. Turn onto wire rack.

Makes 12.

■ Recipe best made close to serving.
■ Freeze: Not suitable.
■ Microwave: Suitable.

ABOVE: From back: Rice and Barley Country Soup, Ham and Zucchini Muffins.

RICE CRISPS

2 cups (300g) rice flour
⅔ cup (80g) soya flour
1 teaspoon ground ginger
2 teaspoons garlic salt
40g butter
2 teaspoons cracked black pepper
⅓ cup (80ml) mild sweet chilli sauce
⅔ cup (160ml) water, approximately

Sift flours, ginger and garlic salt into bowl; rub in butter. Make well in centre, stir in pepper, sauce and enough water to form a soft dough. Place dough into piping bag fitted with star tube. Pipe 5cm lengths of dough onto greased oven trays. Bake in slow oven about 1 hour or until golden brown and dry.

Makes about 100.

- ■ Recipe can be made up to 1 week ahead.
- ■ Storage: Airtight container.
- ■ Freeze: Not suitable.
- ■ Microwave: Not suitable.

RIGHT: Vietnamese Rice Paper Rolls.
BELOW: Rice Crisps.

VIETNAMESE RICE PAPER ROLLS

Rolls can be assembled by each person at the table.

50g rice vermicelli noodles
2 bacon rashers
2 teaspoons warmed honey
1 teaspoon dry sherry
1 small (130g) green cucumber, halved, seeded
8 medium shelled cooked prawns
8 x 22cm round rice paper sheets
1 medium (120g) carrot, grated
¾ cup (60g) bean sprouts
16 mint leaves
8 sprigs fresh coriander

DIPPING SAUCE

**1 teaspoon finely chopped fresh
  lemon grass**
¼ cup (60ml) mild sweet chilli sauce
**1 tablespoon chopped roasted
  unsalted peanuts**
1 tablespoon white vinegar
1 teaspoon chopped fresh mint

Break vermicelli in several places. Cover vermicelli with warm water in bowl, stand 10 minutes; drain well. Brush bacon with combined honey and sherry; grill until cooked, cool; chop. Cut cucumber into long, thin strips. Halve prawns lengthways.

Immerse each sheet of rice paper separately in a bowl of warm water; drain immediately. Covering about a third of each sheet of rice paper, place some noodles, carrot, a strip of cucumber, bean sprouts, 2 prawn halves, 2 mint leaves and bacon.

Partly roll the rice paper to cover filling, fold in sides, add coriander. Continue rolling rice paper to seal. Repeat with remaining rice paper and remaining ingredients. Serve with dipping sauce.
Dipping Sauce: Combine all ingredients in small bowl; mix well.

Makes 8.

■ Can be made several hours ahead.
■ Storage: Covered with damp cloth, in refrigerator.
■ Freeze: Not suitable.
■ Microwave: Not suitable.

DOUBLE RICE PATTIES WITH GARLIC MAYONNAISE

2 bacon rashers, chopped
1 small (80g) onion, chopped
½ cup (100g) arborio rice
¼ cup (45g) wild rice
1½ cups (375ml) chicken stock
¼ cup (60ml) dry white wine
¼ cup (35g) drained chopped
**   sun-dried tomatoes**
¼ cup (20g) grated parmesan cheese
1 tablespoon chopped fresh parsley
2 teaspoons chopped fresh thyme
¼ cup (40g) polenta, approximately
cooking oil spray
rocket leaves

GARLIC MAYONNAISE
1 egg yolk
2 teaspoons lemon juice
½ teaspoon Dijon mustard
1 clove garlic, crushed
1 teaspoon sugar
¼ cup (60ml) olive oil
¼ cup (60ml) light olive oil
1 tablespoon hot water,
**   approximately**

Cook bacon and onion in pan, stirring, until onion is soft. Add all the rice, cook, stirring, 1 minute. Stir in stock and wine, simmer, uncovered, about 20 minutes or until rice is tender, stirring occasionally. Stir in tomatoes, cheese and herbs. Transfer mixture to bowl, cover, refrigerate several hours or until firm.

Blend or process 1 cup of the mixture until smooth. Combine pureed rice mixture with remaining rice mixture. Roll level tablespoons of mixture into balls, flatten slightly, toss in polenta.

Coat oven tray with cooking oil spray, place patties on tray, coat patties with cooking oil spray. Bake, uncovered, in moderately hot oven about 20 minutes or until heated through. Serve with rocket and garlic mayonnaise.

Garlic Mayonnaise: Blend or process egg yolk, juice, mustard, garlic and sugar until smooth. Add combined oils gradually in a thin stream while motor is operating; add enough water to bring mayonnaise to desired consistency. Blend until smooth.

Makes 20.

■ Recipe can be prepared a day ahead.
■ Storage: Covered, in refrigerator.
■ Freeze: Patties suitable.
■ Microwave: Not suitable.

PAELLA CROQUETTES

1 cup (200g) white long-grain rice
2 cups (500ml) chicken stock
1 bay leaf
1 teaspoon ground turmeric
2 teaspoons olive oil
1 clove garlic, crushed
1 medium (170g) red Spanish onion,
**   chopped**
100g chorizo sausage, chopped
100g smoked chicken, chopped
1 tablespoon chopped fresh parsley
plain flour
2 eggs, lightly beaten
1 tablespoon milk
1 cup (100g) packaged breadcrumbs
vegetable oil for deep-frying

Combine rice, stock, bay leaf and turmeric in heavy-based pan, bring to boil, stirring, reduce heat, simmer gently, covered with tight-fitting lid, 12 minutes. Remove from heat, stand, covered, 10 minutes. Fluff rice with fork, discard bay leaf; cool.

Heat olive oil in pan, add garlic, onion and sausage, cook, stirring, until onion is soft; cool. Process rice, sausage mixture, chicken and parsley until ingredients start to cling together. Shape ¼ cups of rice

mixture with wet hands into croquette shapes. Toss croquettes in flour; shake away excess flour. Dip in combined eggs and milk, then in breadcrumbs. Cover, refrigerate 30 minutes. Just before serving, deep-fry croquettes in hot oil until browned and heated through.

Makes about 10.

■ Recipe can be prepared a day ahead.
■ Storage: Covered, in refrigerator.
■ Freeze: Uncooked croquettes suitable.
■ Microwave: Rice suitable.

KUMARA AND AVOCADO ROULADE

30g butter
1 small (80g) onion, finely chopped
1½ cups grated uncooked kumara
2 tablespoons plain flour
4 eggs, separated
¼ cup (20g) grated parmesan cheese

AVOCADO FILLING
2 bacon rashers, finely chopped
2 cups cooked white short-grain rice
½ cup (125ml) mayonnaise
1 small (200g) avocado, chopped
2 tablespoons chopped fresh chives

Grease 25cm x 30cm Swiss roll pan, cover base with baking paper. Heat butter in pan, add onion, cook, stirring, until onion is soft. Add kumara, cook, stirring, until tender. Stir in flour, cool 5 minutes. Stir in egg yolks, transfer mixture to large bowl. Beat egg whites in small bowl with electric mixer until soft peaks form, fold into kumara mixture in 2 batches. Spread mixture into prepared pan, bake in moderately hot oven about 10 minutes or until set.

Turn roulade onto 30cm square piece of baking paper sprinkled with cheese; remove baking paper lining. Carefully spread with avocado filling. Holding paper with both hands, gently lift and roll up from longest side. Serve roulade warm or cold.

Avocado Filling: Cook bacon in pan until crisp; drain on absorbent paper. Combine bacon with remaining ingredients in bowl; mix well.

Serves 4.

■ Recipe can be prepared a day ahead.
■ Storage: Covered, in refrigerator.
■ Freeze: Cooked rice suitable.
■ Microwave: Rice suitable.

LEFT: From left: Double Rice Patties with Garlic Mayonnaise, Paella Croquettes.
BELOW: Kumara and Avocado Roulade.

Below: Glasses from Home & Garden on the Mall.

SPICY CHICKEN WITH SALSA IN RICE CUPS

3 cups cooked white long-grain rice
¼ cup (20g) flaked almonds, toasted
1 egg, lightly beaten
100g mixed lettuce leaves

CORN AND TOMATO SALSA
130g can corn kernels, drained
4 medium (300g) egg tomatoes, seeded, finely chopped
2 green shallots, chopped
2 teaspoons finely chopped glace ginger
1 tablespoon olive oil
1 tablespoon lime juice
2 teaspoons chopped fresh coriander

SPICY CHICKEN
4 single (680g) chicken breast fillets
2 tablespoons tomato sauce
1 tablespoon Worcestershire sauce
1 tablespoon brown sugar
2 teaspoons dry mustard
2 cloves garlic, crushed

Grease 8 holes of 12-hole muffin pan (⅓ cup/80ml capacity). Process rice, nuts and egg until roughly chopped. Divide mixture between holes in prepared pan. Using damp hand, press mixture evenly over base and side of each hole, cover, refrigerate about 1 hour or until rice mixture is firm.

Bake rice cups in moderately hot oven about 30 minutes or until firm and lightly browned. Fill rice cups with corn and tomato salsa, serve with lettuce leaves and spicy chicken.

Corn and Tomato Salsa: Combine all ingredients in bowl; mix well.

Spicy Chicken: Gently pound chicken between sheets of plastic wrap until of even thickness. Combine chicken with remaining ingredients in bowl; mix well. Cover, refrigerate 3 hours or overnight.

Cook undrained chicken on greased griddle pan or barbecue until tender and browned on both sides. Cool 5 minutes before slicing.

Serves 4.

■ Rice cups and salsa can be prepared 3 hours ahead. Chicken can be prepared a day ahead.
■ Storage: Rice cups, at room temperature. Salsa and chicken, covered, in refrigerator.
■ Freeze: Not suitable.
■ Microwave: Rice suitable.

BACON, BEAN AND RICE TACOS

2 teaspoons olive oil
4 green shallots, chopped
2 cloves garlic, crushed
1 small fresh red chilli, finely chopped
2 bacon rashers, chopped
3 medium (225g) egg tomatoes, chopped
½ cup (125ml) tomato puree
1½ cups (375ml) beef stock
35g packet taco seasoning mix
310g can red kidney beans, rinsed, drained
1 cup cooked white long-grain rice
8 x 16cm round tortillas
½ cup (125ml) sour cream
1 medium (250g) avocado, sliced

Heat oil in pan, add shallots, garlic and chilli, cook, stirring, 2 minutes. Add bacon, cook, stirring, 3 minutes. Add tomatoes, puree, stock and seasoning mix, simmer, uncovered, about 10 minutes or until reduced by a third, stir in beans and rice.

Fold tortillas in half, secure with toothpicks to form taco shells. Place on ungreased oven trays, bake in moderate oven about 5 minutes or until heated through. Remove toothpicks. Spoon rice mixture, sour cream and avocado slices into taco shells.

Makes 8.

- Rice filling can be made 2 days ahead.
- Storage: Covered, in refrigerator.
- Freeze: Rice filling suitable.
- Microwave: Rice suitable.

PEACH AND PECAN MUFFINS

1 cup (150g) self-raising flour
1 cup (150g) brown rice flour
1 teaspoon baking powder
1 teaspoon ground cinnamon
¾ cup (165g) caster sugar
¾ cup (90g) chopped pecans
½ cup (130g) chopped drained canned peaches
1 cup (250ml) buttermilk
1 teaspoon vanilla essence
1 egg, lightly beaten

TOPPING
2 tablespoons brown sugar
2 tablespoons rolled rice
20g butter, melted

Grease 12-hole muffin pan (⅓ cup/80ml capacity). Sift flours, baking powder and cinnamon into large bowl, add sugar, nuts

and peaches; mix well. Using a metal spoon, stir in combined buttermilk, essence and egg; mix until just combined. Spoon mixture into prepared pan, sprinkle with topping. Bake in moderately hot oven about 25 minutes or until browned. Turn onto wire rack.

Topping: Combine all ingredients in small bowl; mix well.

Makes 12.

- Recipe best made close to serving time.
- Freeze: Suitable.
- Microwave: Not suitable.

ABOVE: Peach and Pecan Muffins.
ABOVE LEFT: From left: Spicy Chicken with Salsa in Rice Cups, Bacon, Bean and Rice Tacos.

Above left: China, copper dish and tray from Pacific East India Company.

21

LEEK, PROSCIUTTO AND RICE FRITTATA

1 tablespoon olive oil
2 medium (700g) leeks, chopped
3 slices (45g) prosciutto, chopped
7 eggs, lightly beaten
¼ cup (20g) grated parmesan cheese
½ cup (125ml) buttermilk
1 cup cooked white short-grain rice
¼ cup chopped fresh chives

Grease deep 19cm square cake pan. Heat oil in frying pan, add leeks and prosciutto, cook, stirring, until leeks are soft. Combine leek mixture with remaining ingredients in bowl; mix well. Pour mixture into prepared cake pan, bake, uncovered, in moderate oven about 35 minutes or until lightly browned and set. Stand for 5 minutes before turning out.

Serves 4 to 6.

■ Recipe best made just before serving.
■ Freeze: Cooked rice suitable.
■ Microwave: Rice suitable.

CHEESE, NUT AND OLIVE BITELETS

1 cup cooked brown rice
¼ cup (35g) drained chopped sun-dried tomatoes
½ x 250g packet frozen spinach, thawed, well drained
¼ cup (25g) grated mozzarella cheese
2 tablespoons grated parmesan cheese
2 tablespoons pine nuts, toasted
2 tablespoons seedless black olives, chopped
1 teaspoon chopped fresh oregano
275g packet (30 sheets) gow gee wrappers
vegetable oil for deep-frying

Combine rice, tomatoes, spinach, cheeses, nuts, olives and oregano in bowl; mix well. Place rounded teaspoons of mixture on centre of each wrapper. Brush edges lightly with water, pleat edges, bring together in centre, press firmly to seal. Just before serving, deep-fry in hot oil until browned; drain on absorbent paper.

Makes 30.

■ Recipe can be prepared 6 hours ahead.
■ Storage: Covered, in refrigerator.
■ Freeze: Uncooked recipe suitable.
■ Microwave: Rice suitable.

ABOVE: Leek, Prosciutto and Rice Frittata.

Plate from Plumes Gift Agencies.

BUTTERMILK PIKELETS WITH NUTTY PEPPER SALSA

⅔ cup (100g) plain flour
⅔ cup (100g) rice flour
1 teaspoon baking powder
1 egg, lightly beaten
1½ cups (375ml) buttermilk
½ cup cooked brown rice
½ cup cooked white short-grain rice
cooking oil spray

NUTTY PEPPER SALSA
1 medium (200g) red pepper
1 medium (200g) yellow pepper
250g asparagus, chopped
1 tablespoon olive oil
1 medium (150g) onion, sliced
2 medium (150g) egg tomatoes,
    chopped
⅓ cup (50g) pine nuts, toasted

Sift flours and baking powder into bowl, make well in centre, whisk in egg and buttermilk until smooth, stir in all the rice. Cover, stand 1 hour.

Heat heavy-based pan, coat with cooking oil spray, drop 2 tablespoons of mixture into pan, cook until browned on 1 side, turn to brown other side. Repeat with rest of mixture. Serve with nutty pepper salsa.

Nutty Pepper Salsa: Quarter peppers, remove seeds and membranes. Grill peppers, skin side up, until skin blisters and blackens. Peel away skin, slice peppers. Add asparagus to pan of boiling water, cook 1 minute; drain, rinse under cold water, drain. Heat oil in pan, add onion, cook, stirring, until just tender. Add tomatoes, asparagus and peppers, cook, stirring, until any liquid has evaporated. Stir in toasted pine nuts.

Makes about 15.

■ Recipe best made close to serving.
■ Freeze: Cooked pikelets suitable.
■ Microwave: Asparagus and
   rice suitable.

BELOW: From back: Buttermilk Pikelets with Nutty Pepper Salsa, Cheese, Nut and Olive Bitelets.

TRIPLE CHEESE TEMPTERS

2 cups cooked white short-grain rice
3 slices (90g) mortadella,
    finely chopped
60g mozzarella cheese,
    finely chopped
100g blue vein cheese, crumbled
¼ cup (20g) grated parmesan cheese
2 tablespoons chopped fresh chives
1 tablespoon chopped fresh parsley
1 egg, lightly beaten
1 cup (95g) rolled rice flakes,
    approximately
vegetable oil for deep-frying

Combine rice, mortadella, all the cheese, chives, parsley and egg in bowl; mix well. Cover, refrigerate 30 minutes or until firm. Roll level tablespoons of mixture into balls, coat in rice flakes. Deep-fry balls in batches in hot oil until golden brown; drain on absorbent paper.

Makes about 30.

■ Recipe can be prepared a day ahead.
■ Storage: Covered, in refrigerator.
■ Freeze: Cooked rice suitable.
■ Microwave: Rice suitable.

ABOVE: Triple Cheese Tempters.

WILD RICE TRIANGLES WITH CREAMED LEEK TOPPING

250g asparagus
6 slices (90g) prosciutto
3 cups hot cooked white
long-grain rice
1 cup hot cooked wild rice
⅓ cup (25g) grated parmesan cheese
1 egg
1 tablespoon olive oil
20g butter

CREAMED LEEKS
1 tablespoon olive oil
2 large (1kg) leeks, finely sliced
½ cup (125ml) cream

Grease 19cm x 29cm rectangular slice pan, line base and sides with baking paper, extending opposite ends of paper above pan edge. Trim and discard tough ends from asparagus. Cut asparagus in half. Boil, steam or microwave asparagus until just tender; drain, rinse under cold water, drain. Grill prosciutto until crisp, break in half.

Process all the rice, cheese and egg until rice is roughly chopped. Press rice mixture evenly into prepared pan, cover, refrigerate about 1 hour or until firm. Gently remove rice mixture from pan, cut into 6 rectangles, cut each rectangle in half to form 12 triangles.

Heat oil and butter in pan, cook triangles in batches until golden brown on both sides; drain on absorbent paper. Serve wild rice triangles topped with creamed leeks, asparagus and prosciutto.

Creamed Leeks: Heat oil in pan, add leeks, cook, stirring, until leeks are tender. Add cream, cook, stirring, until mixture is slightly thickened.

Serves 6.

- Rice mixture can be prepared a day ahead.
- Storage: Covered, in refrigerator.
- Freeze: Not suitable.
- Microwave: Rice and asparagus suitable.

BELOW: Wild Rice Triangles with Creamed Leek Topping.

Plate from Plumes Gift Agencies: scoop from Morris Home & Garden Wares.

PUFFED RICE CRISPS WITH CHILLI RELISH

4½ cups cooked jasmine rice
vegetable oil for shallow-frying

CHILLI RELISH
1 tablespoon peanut oil
5 small fresh red chillies, chopped
1 large (200g) onion, chopped
2 cloves garlic, crushed
2 medium (400g) red peppers,
   chopped
¼ cup (50g) brown sugar
¼ cup (60ml) cider vinegar
1 teaspoon fish sauce
2 teaspoons lime juice
1 tablespoon chopped fresh
   coriander

Grease 26cm x 32cm Swiss roll pan. Firmly press rice into pan with damp hands. Cook rice in slow oven about 2½ hours or until rice feels dry and crisp. Break rice into pieces, shallow-fry in hot oil on both sides until puffed. Do not allow rice to colour. Serve with chilli relish.

Chilli Relish: Heat oil in pan, add chillies, onion, garlic and peppers, cook, stirring, until onion and peppers are soft. Stir in sugar, vinegar and sauce, cook, stirring, until sugar is dissolved. Simmer 15 minutes or until slightly thickened, stir in juice and coriander; cool. Process mixture until finely chopped.

Serves 6 to 8.

■ Rice can be dried a week ahead. Rice best puffed just before serving. Relish can be made 3 days ahead.
■ Storage: Rice, in airtight container; relish, covered, in refrigerator.
■ Freeze: Not suitable.
■ Microwave: Rice suitable.

RICE AND ARTICHOKE PIZZA WITH RED PESTO

3 bacon rashers, chopped
4½ cups cooked white long-grain rice
½ cup (40g) grated parmesan cheese
100g mozzarella cheese, grated
390g can artichoke hearts,
   drained, quartered
8 seedless black olives, sliced
1 tablespoon chopped fresh chives

RED PESTO
3 medium (600g) red peppers
3 cloves garlic, crushed
⅓ cup (35g) drained sun-dried
   tomatoes
¼ cup (20g) grated parmesan cheese
1 tablespoon drained capers
2 tablespoons pine nuts, toasted
1 medium (130g) tomato,
   roughly chopped

BASIL CREAM
2 tablespoons chopped fresh basil
⅓ cup (80ml) sour cream
⅓ cup (65g) ricotta cheese

Grease 30cm pizza pan. Add bacon to frying pan, cook, stirring, until browned; drain on absorbent paper.

Process rice and parmesan cheese until rice is roughly chopped. Using damp hands, press rice mixture firmly over base of prepared pan, cover, refrigerate about 1 hour or until firm. Bake rice base in moderately hot oven for about 40 minutes or until lightly browned and crisp. Spread red pesto over base, top with bacon,

mozzarella and artichokes. Sprinkle with olives and dot tablespoons of basil cream over pizza. Bake, uncovered, in moderately hot oven about 25 minutes or until cheese is melted. Serve sprinkled with chives.

Red Pesto: Quarter peppers, remove seeds and membranes. Grill peppers, skin side up, until skin blisters and blackens. Peel away skin, roughly chop peppers. Process peppers with remaining ingredients until smooth.

Basil Cream: Combine all ingredients in bowl; mix well.

Serves 4.

■ Pesto can be made a day ahead. Recipe best assembled close to serving.
■ Storage: Covered, in refrigerator.
■ Freeze: Not suitable.
■ Microwave: Rice suitable.

ABOVE: Rice and Artichoke Pizza with Red Pesto.
ABOVE LEFT: Puffed Rice Crisps with Chilli Relish.

Above: Glasses from Freedom Furniture Stores.
Above left: Fabric from Les Olivades.

Main Courses

A simple portion of rice becomes sensational in these main courses, either as the star or mixing unobtrusively with other ingredients. The recipes reflect ideas from around the world, with scrumptious risottos, pilafs and paella — they've never been so good before —and treats ranging from Cantonese-style deep-fried chicken to lamb and rice pies, and special-occasion duck with wild rice and orange mustard sauce. For helpful rice cooking tips, turn to page 120.

PESTO RISOTTO WITH MEATBALLS

1 tablespoon olive oil
1 medium (150g) onion, chopped
1 clove garlic, crushed
¼ cup (40g) pine nuts
1½ cups (300g) arborio rice
½ cup (125ml) dry white wine
3 cups (750ml) chicken stock
⅓ cup chopped fresh basil
½ cup (40g) grated parmesan cheese
⅓ cup (35g) drained sun-dried
    tomatoes, sliced
½ cup (125ml) cream

MEATBALLS
500g minced beef
1 egg, lightly beaten
1 clove garlic, crushed
1 cup (70g) stale breadcrumbs
2 tablespoons tomato paste
2 tablespoons chopped fresh basil
vegetable oil for shallow-frying

Heat oil in large pan, add onion, garlic and nuts, cook, stirring, until onion is soft. Add rice; stir to coat with oil. Stir in wine, simmer, uncovered, stirring, until wine has been absorbed. Stir in stock, simmer, covered, 10 minutes. Remove from heat, stand, covered, 10 minutes. Return to heat, stir in remaining ingredients, stir over heat about 4 minutes or until thick and creamy. Serve risotto with meatballs.
Meatballs: Combine beef, egg, garlic, breadcrumbs, paste and basil in bowl; mix well. Shape rounded teaspoons of mixture into balls. Shallow-fry meatballs in hot oil until browned and cooked through; drain on absorbent paper.
Serves 4.

■ Meatballs can be made a day ahead.
■ Storage: Covered, in refrigerator.
■ Freeze: Meatballs suitable.
■ Microwave: Risotto suitable.

PEPPERONI RISOTTO

150g green beans, halved
1.5 litres (6 cups) chicken stock
2 tablespoons tomato paste
1 tablespoon olive oil
20g butter
1 large (200g) onion, chopped
1 medium (200g) red pepper, chopped
2 cups (400g) arborio rice
200g pepperoni, sliced
⅓ cup (50g) pimiento-stuffed
    green olives

Add beans to large pan of boiling water; drain immediately, rinse under cold water, drain. Combine stock and paste in pan, bring to boil, cover; keep hot.

Heat oil and butter in large pan, add onion and pepper, cook, stirring, until onion is soft. Stir in rice, then 2/3 cup (160ml) of boiling stock mixture, cook, stirring, over low heat until liquid is absorbed. Continue adding stock mixture gradually, stirring until absorbed before each addition. Total cooking time should be about

35 minutes or until rice is tender. Stir in pepperoni, olives and beans, stir until hot. Serves 4.

■ Recipe best made just before serving.
■ Freeze: Not suitable.
■ Microwave: Suitable.

ABOVE: From left: Pepperoni Risotto, Pesto Risotto with Meatballs.

STEAK AND MUSHROOM PIES

2 tablespoons olive oil
1kg beef rump steak, chopped
2 medium (300g) onions, finely chopped
2 bacon rashers, finely chopped
250g button mushrooms, halved
1 teaspoon chopped fresh rosemary
2 bay leaves
½ cup (125ml) dry red wine
½ cup (125ml) port
2½ cups (625ml) beef stock
⅓ cup (65g) white short-grain rice
1 teaspoon cornflour
1 tablespoon water
1 egg, lightly beaten

PASTRY
250g cold butter, chopped
1½ cups (225g) plain flour
1 tablespoon lemon juice, approximately

Heat half the oil in large pan, add beef in batches, cook, stirring, until well browned; remove from pan. Heat remaining oil in pan, add onions, bacon and mushrooms, cook, stirring, until onions are soft. Add rosemary, bay leaves, wine, port and stock. Return beef to pan, simmer, covered, 25 minutes. Stir in rice, simmer 10 minutes. Stir in blended cornflour and water, stir over heat until mixture boils and thickens. Divide mixture between 6 shallow oven-proof dishes (1½ cup/375ml capacity).

Cut pastry into 6 portions, roll pastry until large enough to cover filling, cut 1cm hole in centres. Place pastry over filling, brush pastry with egg. Refrigerate 20 minutes. Stand pies on oven tray, bake in hot oven about 20 minutes or until golden brown.

Pastry: Process butter and flour until mixture resembles breadcrumbs. Add enough juice to make ingredients just come together. Knead lightly on floured surface until smooth, wrap in plastic, refrigerate 30 minutes.

Makes 6.

■ Recipe can be prepared a day ahead.
■ Storage: Covered, in refrigerator.
■ Freeze: Suitable.
■ Microwave: Not suitable.

BEEF STEAK PUDDING WITH BUTTERMILK CRUST

750g blade steak, chopped
1 medium (150g) onion, chopped
2 bacon rashers, chopped
2 medium (400g) old potatoes, chopped
½ cup (125ml) water
125g can condensed tomato soup

BUTTERMILK CRUST
¾ cup (105g) self-raising flour
¼ cup (35g) rice flour
60g lard
¼ cup (60ml) buttermilk
¼ cup chopped fresh parsley
2 tablespoons water, approximately

Combine all ingredients in bowl; mix well. Pour mixture into pudding basin (2 litre/ 8 cup capacity), top with buttermilk crust. Cover with a round of greased baking paper, then lid. Alternatively, cover with foil, tie foil securely. Place basin in large pan with enough boiling water to come halfway up side of basin. Simmer, covered, 3 hours; replenish boiling water as necessary.

Buttermilk Crust: Sift flours into bowl, rub in lard, stir in combined buttermilk and parsley, Add enough water to mix to a soft dough, knead lightly. Press into round shape large enough to cover beef mixture.

Serves 4 to 6.

■ Recipe best made close to serving.
■ Freeze: Not suitable.
■ Microwave: Not suitable.

ABOVE LEFT: From back: Steak and Mushroom Pies, Beef Steak Pudding with Buttermilk Crust.

Setting from Accoutrement.

INDIAN PILAF WITH CRUNCHY MARINATED CHICKEN

2 tablespoons peanut oil
1 large (200g) onion, sliced
2 cloves garlic, crushed
2 teaspoons cumin seeds
2 teaspoons caraway seeds
½ teaspoon ground turmeric
2 cups (400g) basmati rice
1 litre (4 cups) chicken stock
¼ cup (35g) dried currants
2 tablespoons chopped fresh coriander

CRUNCHY MARINATED CHICKEN
750g chicken thigh fillets, halved
⅓ cup (80ml) lime juice
2 cloves garlic, crushed
2 teaspoons grated fresh ginger
2 tablespoons mild sweet chilli sauce
cornflour
vegetable oil for shallow-frying

Heat oil in pan, add onion, garlic, seeds and turmeric, cook, stirring, until onion is soft. Add rice, stir over heat until rice is coated with oil. Stir in stock, simmer, covered, 15 minutes. Remove from heat; stand, covered, further 15 minutes. Stir in currants and coriander; serve with crunchy marinated chicken.

Crunchy Marinated Chicken: Combine chicken, juice, garlic, ginger and sauce in bowl, refrigerate 3 hours or overnight.

Drain chicken; discard marinade. Toss chicken in cornflour; shake away excess cornflour. Shallow-fry chicken in hot oil until browned and tender; drain on absorbent paper.

Serves 6.

■ Recipe best cooked just before serving. Chicken can be marinated a day ahead.
■ Storage: Covered, in refrigerator.
■ Freeze: Uncooked marinated chicken suitable.
■ Microwave: Not suitable.

ABOVE: Indian Pilaf with Crunchy Marinated Chicken.

Indian bowl from Morris Home & Garden Wares.

CHICKEN AND SEAFOOD PAELLA

250g mussels
250g medium uncooked prawns
4 chicken wings
2 tablespoons olive oil
2 (310g) chorizo sausages, thinly
    sliced
2 cups (400g) white long-grain rice
3 green shallots, chopped
1 large (350g) green pepper, chopped
1 large (350g) red pepper, chopped
¼ teaspoon saffron powder
1 tablespoon tomato paste
2½ cups (625ml) vegetable stock
1 cup (250ml) dry white wine
1½ cups (185g) frozen peas
3 medium (225g) egg tomatoes,
    peeled, seeded, chopped
250g firm white fish fillets, chopped
200g calamari rings

Scrub mussels, remove beards. Shell and devein prawns, leaving heads and tails intact. Remove and discard wing tips from chicken. Cut each wing into pieces at each joint.

Heat oil in large pan, add chicken, cook until browned and tender; remove from pan. Add sausages to pan, cook until lightly browned; drain on absorbent paper. Stir in rice, shallots and peppers. Stir in saffron and paste. Add 1 cup (250ml) stock, cook, stirring, until liquid is nearly absorbed. Add wine, cook, stirring, until wine is nearly absorbed. Add remaining stock, cook, stirring, until stock boils. Add mussels, prawns, peas, tomatoes, fish and calamari, cook, covered, over low heat only until mussels open. Add chicken and sausages, simmer, covered, until heated through.

Serves 6 to 8.

■ Recipe best made just before serving.
■ Freeze: Not suitable.
■ Microwave: Not suitable.

Chicken and Seafood Paella.

Platter from N. & N. Catering Enterprises;
basket from Barbara's Storehouse.

ROASTED PEPPER HALVES WITH TOMATO RICE

4 large (1.4kg) red peppers
¼ cup (60ml) olive oil
1 medium (150g) onion, chopped
1 clove garlic, crushed
1½ cups (300g) basmati rice
⅓ cup (80ml) dry white wine
425g can tomatoes
2 cups (500ml) chicken stock
1 tablespoon tomato paste
3 small (270g) zucchini, chopped
2 (120g) finger eggplants, chopped
125g feta cheese, crumbled
1 teaspoon chopped fresh oregano
1 teaspoon chopped fresh basil
2 teaspoons chopped fresh parsley

Halve peppers lengthways, remove seeds and membranes. Brush skin of each pepper with a little of the oil. Place peppers on oven tray, bake, uncovered, in moderate oven 15 minutes. Heat remaining oil in pan, add onion, garlic and rice, cook, stirring, until onion is soft. Add wine, cook, stirring, until wine is absorbed. Stir in undrained crushed tomatoes. Add 1 cup (250ml) of combined stock and paste, cook, stirring, until liquid is absorbed. Stir in remaining stock mixture, zucchini and eggplants, cook, covered, over low heat until liquid is absorbed and vegetables are tender, stirring occasionally. Spoon mixture into roasted peppers. Sprinkle with cheese and herbs. Bake, uncovered, in moderate oven about 20 minutes or until cheese is melted.

Serves 4 to 6.

■ Recipe best made on day of serving.
■ Storage: Covered, in refrigerator.
■ Freeze: Not suitable.
■ Microwave: Not suitable.

COCONUT LAMB CASSEROLE WITH CORIANDER RICE

½ cup (125ml) coconut milk
2 tablespoons lemon juice
1 teaspoon ground cumin
1 teaspoon ground coriander
½ teaspoon ground cinnamon
½ teaspoon cayenne pepper
1.2kg diced lamb
2 tablespoons vegetable oil
1 clove garlic, crushed
2 teaspoons grated fresh ginger
1 medium (150g) onion, chopped
2 x 425g cans tomatoes
1 tablespoon tomato paste
400ml can coconut cream

CORIANDER RICE
1 tablespoon vegetable oil
1 medium (150g) onion, finely chopped
1 teaspoon ground cumin
1 teaspoon ground coriander
1 teaspoon garam masala
½ teaspoon ground turmeric
1½ cups (300g) basmati rice
2 cups (500ml) chicken stock
2 cups (500ml) water
¼ cup (35g) dried currants
½ cup (60g) frozen peas
¾ cup (105g) slivered almonds, toasted
1 tablespoon chopped fresh coriander

Combine coconut milk, juice, spices and lamb in bowl; mix well. Cover, refrigerate 3 hours or overnight.

Heat oil in pan, add garlic, ginger and onion, cook, stirring, until onion is soft. Add lamb in batches, cook, stirring, until

lamb is browned. Return lamb to pan, add undrained crushed tomatoes and paste, simmer, covered, 45 minutes, stirring occasionally. Stir in coconut cream, simmer, uncovered, further 15 minutes or until slightly thickened. Serve casserole with coriander rice.

Coriander Rice: Heat oil in pan, add onion and spices, cook, stirring, until onion is soft. Stir in rice, stock and water, simmer, covered, 10 minutes. Add currants and peas, simmer, covered, further 2 minutes or until rice is tender and liquid absorbed. Stir in nuts and fresh coriander.

Serves 4 to 6.

- ■ Rice best cooked just before serving. Lamb casserole can be made a day ahead.
- ■ Storage: Covered, in refrigerator.
- ■ Freeze: Not suitable.
- ■ Microwave: Not suitable.

LAMB BIRIANI

¼ cup (60ml) vegetable oil
1 medium (150g) onion, chopped
2 cloves garlic, crushed
2 teaspoons tikka curry paste
1 tablespoon mild curry powder
1 teaspoon ground cinnamon
1 teaspoon ground cumin
¼ teaspoon ground cloves
1 tablespoon grated fresh ginger
⅓ cup chopped fresh coriander
500g boned lamb shoulder, chopped
2 cups (400g) basmati rice
1 litre (4 cups) chicken stock
1 cup (125g) frozen peas
310g can corn kernels, drained
⅓ cup (55g) sultanas
⅓ cup (50g) chopped pistachios, toasted
1 medium (130g) tomato, chopped
1 tablespoon chopped fresh coriander, extra

Heat oil in pan, add onion, garlic, paste, spices, ginger and coriander, cook, stirring, until onion is soft. Add lamb, cook, stirring, until lamb is browned. Stir in rice, then stock, cook, covered, stirring occasionally, until almost all liquid is absorbed. Add peas, simmer, covered, until all liquid is absorbed and lamb is cooked. Add corn and sultanas, remove from heat, stand, covered, 10 minutes before serving. Serve sprinkled with nuts, tomato and extra coriander.

Serves 4 to 6.

- ■ Recipe best made just before serving.
- ■ Freeze: Not suitable.
- ■ Microwave: Not suitable.

ABOVE LEFT: Roasted Pepper Halves with Tomato Rice.
ABOVE: From back: Lamb Biriani, Coconut Lamb Casserole with Coriander Rice.

LAMB AND RED PEPPER RICE PASTRIES

2 teaspoons olive oil
8 (500g) lamb fillets
12 sheets fillo pastry
100g butter, melted

RED PEPPER RICE

1 tablespoon olive oil
30g butter
1 medium (170g) red Spanish onion, chopped
100g button mushrooms, sliced
1 medium (200g) red pepper, finely chopped
1 clove garlic, crushed
1 cup (200g) basmati rice
1/2 cup (125ml) dry white wine
2 cups (500ml) beef stock
1 cup (250ml) water
1/3 cup (25g) grated romano cheese
2 tablespoons chopped fresh parsley
1 teaspoon chopped fresh rosemary

Heat oil in pan, add lamb, cook until well browned; drain on absorbent paper. Cut lamb fillets in half.

Layer 3 pastry sheets together, brushing each with butter. Place quarter of the red pepper rice in centre of layered pastry, top with 4 pieces of lamb. Bring edges together in centre, press firmly to seal. Repeat with remaining pastry, butter, red pepper rice and lamb. Place pastries on greased oven tray, bake in moderate oven about 20 minutes or until browned.

Red Pepper Rice: Heat oil and butter in pan, add onion, mushrooms, pepper and garlic, cook, stirring, until onion is soft. Stir in rice and wine, simmer, uncovered, until almost all wine is absorbed. Stir in stock and water, simmer, uncovered, about 15 minutes or until rice is tender, stirring occasionally, stir in cheese and herbs; cool.

Makes 4.

- Red pepper rice can be made a day ahead.
- Storage: Covered, in refrigerator.
- Freeze: Not suitable.
- Microwave: Red pepper rice suitable.

WARM LAMB AND WILD RICE SALAD

3 teaspoons olive oil
8 (500g) lamb fillets
1 clove garlic, crushed
2 1/4 cups cooked brown rice and wild rice blend
1 cup (100g) mung bean sprouts
12 small (120g) radishes, sliced
2 tablespoons chopped fresh mint

DRESSING

1/4 cup (60ml) lime juice
1 tablespoon honey
1 tablespoon olive oil
1 tablespoon soy sauce
1 clove garlic, crushed
2 small fresh red chillies, chopped
1 tablespoon chopped fresh coriander

Heat oil in pan, add lamb and garlic, cook until lamb is well browned; drain on absorbent paper. Cut lamb into 1cm slices. Return lamb to pan, add rice and half the dressing, cook, stirring, until combined. Add sprouts and remaining dressing, stir until hot. Stir in radishes and mint.

Dressing: Combine all ingredients in jar; shake well.

Serves 4.

- Recipe best made close to serving.
- Freeze: Cooked rice suitable.
- Microwave: Rice suitable.

From back: Lamb and Red Pepper Rice Pastries, Warm Lamb and Rice Salad.

Setting from House.

LAYERED RICE CAKE

415g can salmon, drained, flaked
2 cups cooked white long-grain rice
2 green shallots, chopped
2 eggs, lightly beaten
1 teaspoon grated lemon rind

SPINACH LAYER

1 tablespoon olive oil
1 medium (150g) onion, chopped
1 clove garlic, crushed
250g packet frozen chopped
    spinach, thawed
2 cups cooked white long-grain rice
2 eggs, lightly beaten

CHEESE HERB LAYER

2 cups cooked white long-grain rice
1 tablespoon chopped fresh basil
½ cup (40g) grated parmesan cheese
2 eggs, lightly beaten

Combine salmon, rice, shallots, eggs and rind in bowl; mix well. Spread mixture over base of greased 24cm springform tin. Top with spinach layer; then cheese herb layer. Place tin on oven tray. Bake, uncovered, in moderate oven about 45 minutes or until set. Stand 10 minutes before slicing. Serve with mayonnaise and lemon wedges, if desired.

Spinach Layer: Heat oil in pan, add onion, garlic and spinach, cook, stirring, until liquid has evaporated; cool. Combine spinach mixture, rice and eggs in bowl; mix well.

Cheese Herb Layer: Combine all ingredients in bowl; mix well.

Serves 6.

■ Recipe can be made a day ahead.
■ Storage: Covered, in refrigerator.
■ Freeze: Cooked rice suitable.
■ Microwave: Rice suitable.

BRAISED LAMB SHANKS IN SPICED TOMATO SAUCE

2 medium (300g) onions, quartered
4 cloves garlic, crushed
1 tablespoon ground cumin
2 teaspoons ground coriander
2 teaspoons ground turmeric
2 teaspoons ground hot paprika
8 small (2.2kg) lamb shanks
¼ cup (60ml) olive oil
2 x 425g cans tomatoes
1 teaspoon sugar
1 litre (4 cups) water
½ cup (100g) basmati rice
1 bunch (430g) baby carrots
250g frozen broad beans,
    thawed, peeled

Blend or process onions, garlic and spices until smooth. Make 2 small cuts in each shank, place shanks in dish, rub

shanks with half the spice mixture, cover, refrigerate about 3 hours or overnight.

Heat half the oil in large pan, add shanks in batches, cook until browned all over, remove from pan.

Heat remaining oil in pan, add remaining spice mixture, cook, stirring, until fragrant. Add shanks, undrained crushed tomatoes, sugar and water, cook, covered, stirring occasionally, 1¼ hours. Add rice to lamb mixture, cook, covered, 5 minutes, add carrots, cook, covered, 10 minutes or until carrots and rice are tender. Stir in beans, cook, stirring, until heated through.

Serves 4 to 6.

■ Recipe best made close to serving.
■ Freeze: Not suitable.
■ Microwave: Not suitable.

LAMB AND RICE PIES

6 cups cooked white long-grain rice
30g butter
**1½ cups (185g) grated tasty
    cheddar cheese**
**2 tablespoons grated parmesan
    cheese**
1 egg, lightly beaten
1 tablespoon chopped fresh parsley
FILLING
750g lamb neck chops
plain flour
2 tablespoons vegetable oil
1 medium (150g) onion, chopped
1 medium (120g) carrot, sliced
1 stick celery, sliced
125g flat mushrooms, chopped
1 cup (250ml) chicken stock
425g can tomatoes
1 bay leaf
2 tablespoons cornflour
1 tablespoon water
1 tablespoon chopped fresh parsley

Combine warm rice with butter, cheeses and egg; mix well. Press ¾ cup of mixture over base and sides of 6 x 11cm pie dishes (1cup/250ml capacity).

Spread filling into rice shells. Press remaining rice around edge of each dish, leaving a 2cm circle in the centre. Place pies on oven tray, bake in moderately hot oven about 40 minutes or until browned. Sprinkle centres with parsley.

Filling: Remove bones from chops, cut meat into 1cm pieces. Toss meat in flour, shake away excess flour.

Heat oil in pan, add lamb and onion, cook, stirring, until lamb is browned. Add carrot, celery and mushrooms, cover, cook until vegetables are tender. Stir in stock, undrained crushed tomatoes and bay leaf, simmer, covered, about 45 minutes or until lamb is tender. Add blended cornflour and water, stir until mixture boils and thickens, stir in parsley.

Makes 6.

■ Filling can be made a day ahead.
■ Storage: Covered, in refrigerator.
■ Freeze: Cooked filling suitable.
■ Microwave: Rice suitable.

ABOVE LEFT: Layered Rice Cake.
ABOVE: From left: Lamb and Rice Pies, Braised Lamb Shanks in Spiced Tomato Sauce.

Above and left: Plates from The Bay Tree Kitchen Shop.

CURRIED RICE AND LENTILS WITH FRIED ONIONS

20g ghee
2 cloves garlic, crushed
2 teaspoons grated fresh ginger
1 medium (150g) onion, sliced
2 teaspoons garam masala
1 teaspoon cumin seeds
½ teaspoon ground turmeric
1½ cups (300g) basmati rice
1½ cups (300g) red lentils
1.25 litres (5 cups) hot water
**2 medium (260g) tomatoes, peeled,
  seeded, chopped**
**2 tablespoons chopped fresh
  coriander**

FRIED ONIONS
vegetable oil for shallow-frying
2 medium (300g) onions, finely sliced

Heat ghee in pan, add garlic, ginger and onion, cook, stirring, until onion is soft. Add spices, rice and lentils, cook, stirring, 3 minutes. Stir in water and tomatoes, simmer, covered, over low heat about 12 minutes or until rice and lentils are tender. Stir in coriander. Serve with fried onions.

Fried Onions: Heat oil in pan, shallow-fry onions in small batches until browned and crisp; drain on absorbent paper.

Serves 4.

■ Recipe best made just before serving.
■ Freeze: Not suitable.
■ Microwave: Curried rice suitable.

CHICKPEA AND RICE BALL CURRY

**5 small fresh green chillies,
  seeded, chopped**
1 teaspoon grated lime rind
**1 teaspoon chopped fresh
  lemon grass**
¼ teaspoon grated fresh ginger
1 clove garlic, crushed
2 fresh coriander roots, chopped
¼ teaspoon ground turmeric
5 black peppercorns
¼ teaspoon belacan
3 teaspoons fish sauce
2 teaspoons vegetable oil
425ml can coconut milk
4 fresh kaffir lime leaves

CHICKPEA AND RICE BALLS

1 tablespoon vegetable oil
1 medium (150g) onion,
   finely chopped
1 clove garlic, crushed
1 teaspoon ground cumin
1 teaspoon ground coriander
310g can chickpeas, rinsed, drained
1 cup cooked jasmine rice
1 tablespoon lemon juice
1 tablespoon chopped fresh basil

Blend or process chillies, rind, lemon grass, ginger, garlic, coriander roots, turmeric, peppercorns, belacan and 1 teaspoon of fish sauce until smooth. Heat oil in pan, add chilli mixture, cook, stirring, until fragrant. Stir in coconut milk and lime leaves, bring to boil, add chickpea and rice balls, simmer, uncovered, about 15 minutes or until sauce is thickened slightly, stirring occasionally. Stir in remaining fish sauce. Discard lime leaves before serving.

Chickpea and Rice Balls: Heat oil in pan, add onion, garlic, cumin and coriander, cook, stirring, until onion is soft. Process onion mixture and remaining ingredients until smooth. Shape mixture into 16 balls.

Serves 4.

- Chickpea and rice balls can be made a day ahead.
- Storage: Covered, in refrigerator.
- Freeze: Cooked rice suitable.
- Microwave: Rice suitable.

FRIED RICE BALLS

2½ cups (625ml) beef stock
1 cup (200g) arborio rice
⅓ cup (25g) grated parmesan cheese
1 egg, lightly beaten
2 tablespoons finely chopped
   drained sun-dried tomatoes
1 tablespoon olive oil
1 small (80g) onion, finely chopped
1 clove garlic, crushed
250g minced veal
½ teaspoon dried oregano leaves
1 tablespoon tomato paste
80g mozzarella cheese
plain flour
1 egg, lightly beaten, extra
2 teaspoons water
1 cup (70g) stale breadcrumbs
vegetable oil for deep-frying

Bring stock to boil in large pan, stir in rice, simmer, covered, about 15 minutes or until liquid is absorbed. Cool 10 minutes. Stir in parmesan cheese, egg and tomatoes.

Heat olive oil in pan, add onion and garlic, cook, stirring, until onion is soft. Add veal, oregano and paste, cook, stirring, until veal is browned and liquid evaporated. Combine rice mixture and veal mixture in bowl; cool.

Cut mozzarella cheese into 8 pieces. With wet hands, shape about a third of a cup of rice mixture into an oval around a piece of cheese. Repeat with remaining

rice and mozzarella cheese. Place ovals on tray, refrigerate 30 minutes.

Dust rice balls in flour, shake away excess flour; dip in combined extra egg and water, roll in breadcrumbs. Deep-fry rice balls in hot vegetable oil until browned; drain on absorbent paper.

Makes 8.

- Recipe can be prepared a day ahead.
- Storage: Covered, in refrigerator.
- Freeze: Not suitable.
- Microwave: Not suitable.

SALMON RICE PATTIES WITH TARTARE SAUCE

415g can salmon, drained, flaked
1 cup cooked brown rice
¾ cup (45g) stale breadcrumbs
2 teaspoons chopped fresh dill
1 teaspoon grated lemon rind
2 green shallots, chopped
1 medium (130g) tomato,
   peeled, chopped
1 egg, lightly beaten
plain flour
vegetable oil for shallow-frying

TARTARE SAUCE
1 egg yolk
¼ teaspoon Dijon mustard
2 teaspoons lime juice
½ cup (125ml) vegetable oil
1 teaspoon drained capers, chopped
2 teaspoons chopped fresh chives
1 green shallot, finely chopped

Combine salmon, rice, breadcrumbs, dill, rind, shallots, tomato and egg in medium bowl; mix well. Shape mixture into 8 patties. Toss patties in flour, shake away excess flour. Shallow-fry patties in hot oil until browned; drain on absorbent paper. Serve with tartare sauce.

Tartare Sauce: Whisk egg yolk, mustard and juice together in bowl, gradually whisk in oil in a thin stream. Stir in capers, chives and shallot.

Serves 4.

- Patties can be prepared a day ahead. Cook just before serving. Tartare sauce can be made 2 days ahead.
- Storage: Covered, separately, in refrigerator.
- Freeze: Cooked rice suitable.
- Microwave: Rice suitable.

LEFT: From back: Currried Rice and Lentils with Fried Onions, Chickpea and Rice Ball Curry.
ABOVE: From left: Salmon Rice Patties with Tartare Sauce, Fried Rice Balls.

Left: Plates from Accoutrement. Above: Plates from Plumes Gift Agencies; metal pot and bottle openers from Morris Home & Garden Wares.

SEASONED SPATCHCOCKS WITH PORT SAUCE

350g sausage mince
1 medium (150g) onion,
   finely chopped
2 cloves garlic, crushed
1 tablespoon chopped fresh thyme
⅓ cup chopped fresh parsley
1 medium (620g) fennel bulb, grated
2 tablespoons dried currants
½ cup cooked brown rice
½ cup cooked wild rice
1 egg, lightly beaten
4 x 500g spatchcocks

PORT SAUCE
2 x 410ml cans chicken consomme
1 small (80g) onion, chopped
1 small (70g) carrot, finely chopped
1 sprig fresh thyme
1 tablespoon cornflour
2 tablespoons water
1½ tablespoons port

Heat non-stick pan, add sausage mince, cook, stirring, until browned and cooked through, remove from pan. Add onion, garlic, herbs, fennel and currants to same pan, cook, stirring, until vegetables are tender. Combine vegetable mixture, mince, all the rice and egg in bowl; mix well.

Fill spatchcocks with seasoning, secure openings with toothpicks, tie legs together, tuck wings under. Place spatchcocks on wire rack in baking dish. Bake, uncovered, in moderately hot oven about 1 hour or until browned and tender. Serve spatchcocks with port sauce.

Port Sauce: Combine consomme, onion, carrot and thyme in medium pan, simmer, uncovered, until mixture is reduced to 2 cups (500ml), strain, discard vegetables and thyme. Return liquid to pan, add blended cornflour and water, cook, stirring, until mixture boils and thickens slightly, stir in port.

Serves 8.

- Port sauce can be made a day ahead.
- Storage: Covered, in refrigerator.
- Freeze: Port sauce and cooked rice suitable.
- Microwave: Port sauce and rice suitable.

ABOVE: Seasoned Spatchcocks with Port Sauce.

Setting from The Bay Tree Kitchen Shop.

CHICKEN AND COCONUT CURRY IN RICE NESTS

1.5kg chicken thigh fillets
2 tablespoons Madras curry paste
2 tablespoons lime juice
1 tablespoon peanut oil
1 cup (250ml) chicken stock
1½ cups (375ml) coconut milk
1 tablespoon mango chutney
300g green beans, sliced
2 teaspoons cornflour
1 tablespoon water
4 green shallots, sliced
1 medium (430g) mango, chopped

RICE NESTS
3 cups (750ml) water
2 x 3cm pieces lime rind
3 cardamom pods
pinch ground turmeric
2 cups (400g) jasmine rice
2 egg whites

Cut chicken into 2cm strips. Combine chicken, paste and juice in bowl; mix well. Cover, refrigerate several hours or overnight.

Heat oil in pan, add chicken in batches, cook, stirring, until browned all over, remove from pan. Drain any excess oil from pan. Return chicken to pan, add stock, coconut milk and chutney, simmer, uncovered, 30 minutes. Add beans and blended cornflour and water, stir over heat until mixture boils and thickens, then simmer, uncovered, about 5 minutes or until beans are tender.

Place rice nests on serving plates, fill with chicken and coconut curry, top with shallots and mango.

Rice Nests: Combine water, rind, cardamom and turmeric in pan, bring to boil. Add rice, reduce heat to low, cover, cook about 12 minutes or until liquid has been absorbed. Discard rind and cardamom. Cool 10 minutes, stir in egg whites.

Grease 6 metal pie dishes (¾ cup/ 180ml capacity), cover bases with baking paper. Press ¾ cup of rice mixture over base and side of each dish, place on oven tray, bake in moderate oven about 20 minutes or until set. Cool 10 minutes.

Makes 6.

- Recipe can be prepared a day ahead.
- Storage: Covered, separately, in refrigerator.
- Freeze: Chicken and coconut curry suitable.
- Microwave: Rice suitable.

BELOW: Chicken and Coconut Curry in Rice Nests.

Plate from Accoutrement.

BEEF CASSEROLE WITH SPICY RICE DUMPLINGS

2 tablespoons vegetable oil
1kg beef chuck steak, chopped
30g butter
12 small (300g) onions
2 cloves garlic, crushed
¼ cup (35g) plain flour
1½ cups (375ml) beef stock
1½ cups (375ml) tomato puree
½ cup (125ml) dry red wine
2 teaspoons Worcestershire sauce
2 teaspoons chopped fresh sage

SPICY RICE DUMPLINGS
1 cup (150g) self-raising flour
½ cup cooked white long-grain rice
½ cup cooked brown rice
60g cold butter, grated
2 tablespoons chopped fresh parsley
1 teaspoon paprika
½ teaspoon sambal oelek
½ cup (125ml) milk, approximately

Heat oil in pan, add steak in batches, cook until well browned; remove from pan. Heat butter in pan, add onions and garlic, cook, stirring, 2 minutes. Add flour, cook, stirring, until flour is lightly browned. Remove from heat, gradually stir in stock, puree and wine, stir over heat until mixture boils and thickens. Add steak, simmer, uncovered, 10 minutes. Stir in sauce and sage. Pour mixture into 2.5 litre (10 cup capacity) casserole dish. Bake, covered, in moderate oven about 1¼ hours or until beef is tender. Top with rounded tablespoons of dumpling mixture, bake, uncovered, in moderately hot oven about 25 minutes or until dumplings are cooked.
Spicy Rice Dumplings: Sift flour into bowl, add all the rice, butter, parsley, paprika and sambal oelek. Add enough milk to mix to a soft dough.

Serves 6.

■ Recipe can be made a day ahead.
■ Storage: Covered, in refrigerator.
■ Freeze: Suitable.
■ Microwave: Rice suitable.

CRUNCHY-TOPPED SAUSAGE AND PEPPER CASSEROLE

2 large (700g) red peppers
1 large (350g) yellow pepper
8 (800g) thick pork sausages
2 teaspoons olive oil
2 large (400g) onions, thinly sliced
200g pepperoni, sliced
2 cloves garlic, crushed
1 tablespoon chopped fresh thyme
⅓ cup (80ml) dry red wine
425g can tomatoes
425g can tomato puree

CRUNCHY TOPPING
40g butter
2 cloves garlic, crushed
1 tablespoon chopped fresh rosemary
2 tablespoons chopped fresh parsley
1 cup (70g) stale breadcrumbs
4 cups cooked white long-grain rice
2 eggs, lightly beaten
1¼ cups (100g) grated parmesan cheese

Quarter peppers, remove seeds and membranes. Grill peppers, skin side up, until skin blisters and blackens. Peel away skin, cut peppers into thin strips.

Prick sausages all over with fork. Heat oil in large pan, add sausages, cook, turning occasionally, until browned all over; drain on absorbent paper; cool.

Slice sausages. Remove all but 1 tablespoon of oil from pan, add onions, pepperoni, garlic and thyme, cook, stirring, until onions are soft. Add wine, undrained crushed tomatoes and puree to onion mixture, cook, uncovered, about 10 minutes or until sauce has thickened slightly; stir in sausages and peppers.

Spoon sausage mixture into shallow ovenproof dish (2 litre/8 cup capacity), top with tablespoons of crunchy topping. Bake, uncovered, in moderately hot oven about 40 minutes or until browned.
Crunchy Topping: Heat butter in pan, add garlic and herbs, cook, stirring, until fragrant. Process garlic mixture, breadcrumbs, rice, eggs and cheese until mixture is roughly chopped and sticky.

Serves 6.

■ Recipe can be prepared a day ahead.
■ Storage: Covered, in refrigerator.
■ Freeze: Suitable.
■ Microwave: Not suitable.

From back: Beef Casserole with Spicy Rice Dumplings, Crunchy-Topped Sausage and Pepper Casserole.

FRUIT AND NUT VEAL PILAF

1 tablespoon olive oil
1 large (300g) red Spanish onion, sliced
2 cups (400g) white long-grain rice
1 litre (4 cups) chicken stock
1 cinnamon stick
3 cloves
20g butter
⅓ cup (50g) pine nuts
¼ cup (35g) slivered almonds
¼ teaspoon allspice
5 (40g) fresh dates, sliced
2 tablespoons (30g) dried apricots, sliced
500g minced veal

Heat oil in heavy-based pan, add onion and rice, cook, stirring, 2 minutes. Stir in stock, cinnamon and cloves, simmer, covered, 12 minutes. Remove from heat, stand, covered, about 5 minutes or until liquid is absorbed and rice tender; discard cinnamon and cloves.

Heat butter in pan, add nuts, stir until browned, add allspice and fruit, cook, stirring, 2 minutes. Add veal, cook, stirring, until veal is tender. Mound rice on platter, surround with veal mixture.

Serves 4.

■ Recipe best made just before serving.
■ Freeze: Veal mixture suitable.
■ Microwave: Suitable.

CREAMY CHICKEN AND ASPARAGUS PASTRIES

3 sheets ready-rolled puff pastry
1 egg yolk
1 tablespoon milk
2 teaspoons sesame seeds

FILLING
1 tablespoon olive oil
400g chicken thigh fillets, sliced
1 small (200g) leek, sliced
250g asparagus, chopped
2 cups cooked white long-grain rice
½ cup (125ml) cream
2 teaspoons French mustard
1 teaspoon chopped fresh thyme
¼ cup (60ml) cream, extra

Cut each sheet of pastry in half diagonally. Place one sixth of the filling in centre of each triangle. Brush edges of pastry with some of the combined egg yolk and milk, fold pastry over filling to form a triangle, press edges together to seal.

Place pastries on greased oven tray, brush with more combined egg yolk and milk, sprinkle with seeds. Bake in hot oven 10 minutes, reduce heat to moderately hot, bake 10 minutes or until browned.

Filling: Heat oil in pan, add chicken, cook, stirring, until browned. Stir in leek, cook, stirring, until leek is soft. Stir in asparagus, rice, cream, mustard and thyme, stir over heat until asparagus is just tender and mixture is thick, stir in extra cream; cool.

Makes 6.

■ Filling can be made a day ahead.
■ Storage: Covered, in refrigerator.
■ Freeze: Suitable.
■ Microwave: Rice suitable.

ABOVE: Fruit and Nut Veal Pilaf.

Setting from Accoutrement.

SMOKED FISH AND RICE STRUDELS

500g smoked fish
2 tablespoons vegetable oil
1 medium (150g) onion, chopped
200g mushrooms, chopped
2 sticks celery, chopped
1 teaspoon sambal oelek
1½ cups cooked white long-grain rice
1 egg, lightly beaten
1 tablespoon chopped fresh dill
½ teaspoon grated lemon rind
12 sheets fillo pastry
100g butter, melted
4 hard-boiled eggs

Remove skin from fish. Place fish in pan, cover with water, simmer 3 minutes; drain, flake fish, discard any bones. Heat oil in pan, add onion, mushrooms, celery and sambal oelek, cook, stirring, until onion is soft. Combine fish, onion mixture, rice, egg, dill and rind in bowl; mix well.

Layer 3 pastry sheets together, brushing each with butter. Spread quarter of rice mixture into 16cm square at 1 end of pastry, top with a boiled egg, roll pastry around filling, tucking in ends, brush with a little more butter. Repeat with remaining pastry, butter, rice mixture and hard-boiled eggs. Decorate with extra pastry cut into fish shapes, if desired. Place strudels onto greased oven tray, bake, uncovered, in moderate oven about 30 minutes or until golden brown.

Serves 4.

- ■ Rice mixture can be made a day ahead.
- ■ Storage: Covered, in refrigerator.
- ■ Freeze: Cooked rice suitable.
- ■ Microwave: Rice suitable.

BELOW: From back: Creamy Chicken and Asparagus Pastries, Smoked Fish and Rice Strudels.

PORK WITH FRUITY RICE

2 teaspoons vegetable oil
1 bacon rasher, chopped
1 small (80g) onion, chopped
1 small (70g) carrot, finely chopped
2 tablespoons orange juice
1 small (130g) apple, grated
1 teaspoon grated orange rind
1 teaspoon grated lemon rind
¼ cup (50g) chopped prunes
½ cup (50g) walnuts, toasted, chopped
½ cup cooked glutinous rice
1 egg, lightly beaten
1.5kg pork neck
2 tablespoons vegetable oil, extra
2 teaspoons plain flour
1 cup (250ml) water
⅓ cup (80ml) dry sherry

Heat oil in pan, add bacon, onion and carrot, cook, stirring, until onion is soft. Add juice and apple, cook, stirring, until liquid has evaporated; cool. Combine onion mixture with rinds, prunes, nuts, rice and egg; mix well.

Place pork on bench, make a cut down centre of pork lengthways, without cutting through end. Cut evenly from centre to 1 side of pork to create a flap. Repeat on other side. Place flaps out to sides of pork, spoon seasoning along centre of pork, roll up firmly, secure with string.

Add extra oil to baking dish, roll pork in oil until well coated. Bake, uncovered, in hot oven 10 minutes, reduce heat to moderate, bake about 1½ hours or until pork is tender.

Remove pork from baking dish; keep warm. Discard all but about 1 tablespoon of pan juices, add flour to dish, stir over heat until bubbling. Gradually stir in water and sherry, stir over heat until sauce boils and thickens.

Serves 6.

■ Recipe best made just before serving.
■ Freeze: Uncooked seasoned pork suitable.
■ Microwave: Rice suitable.

BELOW: Pork with Fruity Rice.

GOUGERE WITH SMOKED SALMON KEDGEREE FILLING

125g butter, chopped
1½ cups (375ml) water
1½ cups (225g) plain flour
6 eggs
¼ cup (20g) grated parmesan cheese
1 tablespoon chopped fresh dill
1 tablespoon chopped fresh chives
2 hard-boiled eggs, quartered

FILLING
250g asparagus, chopped
60g butter
1 tablespoon vegetable oil
1 medium (150g) onion, chopped
1½ cups cooked white long-grain rice
125g sliced smoked salmon
⅓ cup (80ml) cream
1 tablespoon chopped fresh dill
1 tablespoon chopped fresh chives

Combine butter and water in pan, stir until butter has melted and mixture boils. Add flour all at once, stir vigorously over heat until mixture leaves side of pan. Transfer mixture to small bowl of electric mixer. Add eggs 1 at a time, beat on low speed until smooth; stir in cheese and herbs.

Spoon mixture into piping bag fitted with a fluted tube. Pipe pastry onto sides of 4 shallow ovenproof dishes (1½ cup/375ml capacity), leaving a hollow in the centre. Place dishes on oven tray, bake in hot oven about 25 minutes or until browned. Reduce heat to moderate, bake 10 minutes. Spoon filling into hollow, bake further 10 minutes or until filling is heated through. Serve topped with hard-boiled eggs.

Filling: Boil, steam or microwave asparagus until just tender. Heat butter and oil in pan, add onion, cook, stirring, until onion is soft. Add asparagus and rice,

cook, stirring, 2 minutes. Stir in salmon, cream and herbs.

Serves 4.

- Filling can be prepared a day ahead.
- Storage: Covered, in refrigerator.
- Freeze: Cooked rice suitable.
- Microwave: Rice and asparagus suitable.

ABOVE: Gougere with Smoked Salmon Kedgeree Filling.

Wooden tray from Accoutrement.

ROAST QUAIL WITH RICE AND APRICOT SEASONING

12 quail
1 tablespoon vegetable oil
2 strips orange rind, finely sliced
2 cups (500ml) chicken stock
1 cup (250ml) dry white wine
⅓ cup (80ml) port
⅓ cup (65g) firmly packed
    brown sugar
2 teaspoons cornflour

RICE AND APRICOT SEASONING
2 cups cooked white long-grain rice
½ cup cooked wild rice
⅔ cup (100g) chopped dried apricots
12 (120g) slices pancetta, chopped
2 eggs, lightly beaten
¼ cup chopped fresh mint
¼ cup chopped fresh chives

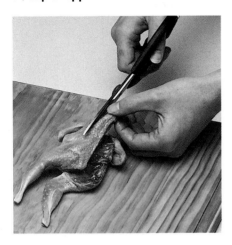

Using scissors or sharp knife, cut along each side of quail backbone; remove and discard bone. Repeat with remaining quail.

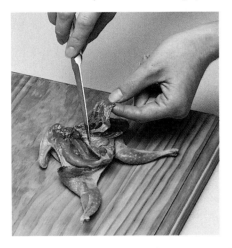

Place quail, skin side down, on board. Carefully cut through thigh joints and wing joints without cutting skin. Scrape meat away from rib cage. Continue scraping meat from rib cage and breastbone, remove and discard bones. Fill quail with rice and apricot seasoning, secure openings with toothpicks, tie legs together, tuck wings under.

Heat oil in baking dish, add quail, cook until browned all over. Pour combined rind, stock, wine, port and sugar over quail. Bake, uncovered, in moderate oven about 20 minutes or until tender; drain, reserve pan juices. Blend cornflour with a tablespoon of pan juices in medium pan, stir in remaining juices. Simmer, stirring, until sauce is reduced to 1 cup (250ml). Serve quail with sauce.
Rice and Apricot Seasoning: Combine all ingredients in bowl; mix well.

Serves 6.

■ Quail can be prepared a day ahead.
■ Storage: Covered, in refrigerator.
■ Freeze: Seasoned quails suitable.
■ Microwave: Rice suitable.

OREGANO CHICKEN WITH CHEESY RICE TOPPING

6 (1kg) single chicken breast fillets
2 cloves garlic, crushed
2 tablespoons lemon juice
1 tablespoon chopped fresh oregano
2 tablespoons olive oil

CHEESY RICE TOPPING
2 cups cooked white long-grain rice
1 egg yolk
½ cup (60g) grated tasty cheddar cheese
½ cup (40g) grated parmesan cheese
60g butter, melted

TOMATO HERB SAUCE
2 teaspoons olive oil
1 clove garlic, crushed
425g can tomatoes
¼ cup (60ml) dry red wine
½ cup (125ml) water
1 teaspoon sugar
1 teaspoon chopped fresh oregano

Combine chicken with garlic, juice, oregano and half the oil in bowl, cover, refrigerate several hours or overnight.

Heat remaining oil in pan, add chicken, cook until browned on both sides and tender. Spread 1 side of each warm chicken breast with topping, grill until browned. Serve with tomato herb sauce.
Cheesy Rice Topping: Process all ingredients until combined.
Tomato Herb Sauce: Heat oil in pan, add garlic, cook, stirring, until fragrant. Stir in undrained crushed tomatoes and remaining ingredients, simmer, uncovered, until slightly thickened.

Serves 6.

■ Sauce can be made 3 days ahead.
■ Storage: Covered, in refrigerator.
■ Freeze: Sauce suitable.
■ Microwave: Sauce and rice suitable.

From back: Roast Quail with Rice and Apricot Seasoning, Oregano Chicken with Cheesy Rice Topping.

China from Waterford Wedgwood; bowl, bird and wooden spoon from Morris Home & Garden Wares.

Rinse slices under cold water; drain, pat dry with absorbent paper. Place slices in single layer on oven trays.

Combine oil, capers, sauce, vinegar and parsley in small bowl, brush 1 side of eggplant slices with caper mixture, grill until lightly browned on both sides.

Place 2 noodle sheets over base of prepared dish, trim another noodle sheet to fit any gaps at side of dish. Sprinkle with quarter of the parmesan; top with half the eggplant slices, more noodle sheets and another quarter of the parmesan. Spread lamb filling over the noodles, top with more noodles and another quarter of the parmesan. Add remaining eggplant slices, top with remaining noodles and remaining cheeses, sprinkle with nuts.

Bake, covered, in moderately hot oven 30 minutes, remove cover, bake about 15 minutes or until heated through and lightly browned.

Lamb Filling: Heat oil in pan, add lamb, cook, stirring, until browned. Add onion, garlic and rosemary, cook, stirring, until onion is soft. Add undrained crushed tomatoes and paste, cook, stirring occasionally, about 10 minutes or until mixture has thickened slightly. Remove from heat, stir in nuts and mint.

Serves 6 to 8.

- Lamb filling can be made a day ahead.
- Storage: Covered, in refrigerator.
- Freeze: Not suitable.
- Microwave: Not suitable.

RICE POLENTA WITH MUSHROOM CREAM SAUCE

1/2 cup (100g) white short-grain rice
2 1/2 cups (625ml) vegetable stock
1 1/2 cups (375ml) milk
1/2 cup (85g) polenta
1/2 cup (40g) grated romano cheese
1/4 cup (40g) pine nuts, toasted, chopped
2 tablespoons chopped fresh basil
1/3 cup (55g) polenta, extra
vegetable oil for shallow-frying

MUSHROOM CREAM SAUCE
2 tablespoons vegetable oil
60g butter
200g button mushrooms
200g flat mushrooms, quartered
200g cremini mushrooms
6 small (60g) spring onions, halved
1 clove garlic, crushed
2 teaspoons cornflour
1/4 cup (60ml) dry white wine
1/2 cup (125ml) beef stock
1/2 cup (125ml) cream
1/2 cup (100g) canned chickpeas, rinsed, drained

Grease deep 19cm square cake pan, line base and 2 opposite sides with baking paper. Combine rice, stock and milk in pan, bring to boil, gradually add polenta, simmer, uncovered, about 10 minutes or until mixture is thick and rice tender, stirring occasionally. Stir in cheese, nuts and

LAMB, RICE AND ALMOND CASSEROLE

2 tablespoons vegetable oil
1kg diced lamb
2 medium (300g) onions, sliced
2 cloves garlic, crushed
2 teaspoons chopped fresh thyme
1 teaspoon ground cumin
1 cup (250ml) dry white wine
1 litre (4 cups) beef stock
2 teaspoons grated lemon rind
1 tablespoon tomato paste
1/3 cup (55g) raisins
1/2 cup (100g) basmati rice
1/3 cup (55g) blanched almonds, toasted
2 tablespoons chopped fresh parsley

Heat oil in pan, add lamb in batches, cook until browned, remove from pan. Add onions, garlic, thyme and cumin to pan, cook, stirring, until onions are soft. Return lamb to pan, stir in wine, stock, rind and paste, simmer, covered, about 50 minutes or until lamb is tender. Stir in raisins and rice, simmer 15 minutes or until rice is tender. Sprinkle with nuts and parsley.

Serves 4.

- Recipe can be made a day ahead.
- Storage: Covered, in refrigerator.
- Freeze: Suitable.
- Microwave: Not suitable.

LAMB AND RICE NOODLE LASAGNE

3 medium (900g) eggplants
coarse cooking salt
1/2 cup (125ml) olive oil
2 tablespoons drained capers, finely chopped
1 tablespoon tomato sauce
1 tablespoon red wine vinegar
1/4 cup chopped fresh parsley
1kg packet rice noodle sheets
1 cup (80g) grated parmesan cheese
1/2 cup (60g) grated tasty cheddar cheese
1 tablespoon pine nuts, toasted

LAMB FILLING
1 tablespoon olive oil
800g minced lamb
1 large (200g) onion, sliced
2 cloves garlic, crushed
1 tablespoon chopped fresh rosemary
425g can tomatoes
1/2 cup (125ml) tomato paste
1 tablespoon pine nuts, toasted
1/4 cup shredded fresh mint

Grease 22cm x 32cm (3 litre/12 cup capacity) rectangular ovenproof dish. Cut eggplants into 5mm slices, place on wire rack, sprinkle with salt, stand 30 minutes.

basil. Spread mixture evenly into prepared pan, cover, refrigerate until firm.

Cut polenta into 8 triangles, coat the triangles in extra polenta. Shallow-fry triangles in hot oil in batches until browned; drain on absorbent paper. Serve triangles with mushroom cream sauce.

Mushroom Cream Sauce: Heat oil and butter in pan, add mushrooms, onions and garlic, cook, stirring, until onions are soft. Stir in blended cornflour and wine,

then stock, stir until sauce boils and thickens slightly. Stir in cream and chickpeas, simmer until heated through.

Serves 4.

■ Polenta triangles can be prepared a day ahead.
■ Storage: Covered, in refrigerator.
■ Freeze: Uncooked polenta suitable.
■ Microwave: Sauce suitable.

LEFT: From back: Lamb, Rice and Almond Casserole, Lamb and Rice Noodle Lasagne.

ABOVE: Rice Polenta with Mushroom Cream Sauce.

Left: Setting from The Bay Tree Kitchen Shop.

CHEESY RICE, PEPPER AND EGGPLANT CASSEROLE

1 large (500g) eggplant
coarse cooking salt
⅓ cup (80ml) olive oil
1 tablespoon olive oil, extra
1 medium (150g) onion, sliced
2 cloves garlic, crushed
2 small (180g) zucchini, sliced
1 medium (200g) red pepper, chopped
1 medium (200g) yellow pepper, chopped
150g mushrooms, chopped
2 medium (260g) tomatoes, chopped
425g can tomato puree
1 tablespoon shredded fresh basil
4½ cups cooked white short-grain rice
¾ cup (75g) grated mozzarella cheese

TOPPING
½ cup (125ml) cream
250g mascarpone cheese
200g ricotta cheese
½ cup (40g) grated parmesan cheese
¼ teaspoon ground nutmeg

Cut eggplant into 5mm slices, place on wire rack, sprinkle with salt, stand 30 minutes. Rinse slices under cold water; drain, pat dry with absorbent paper. Brush eggplant slices with oil, place in single layer on oven trays, grill on both sides until lightly browned.

Heat extra oil in pan, add onion and garlic, cook, stirring, until onion is soft. Add zucchini, peppers, mushrooms and tomatoes, cook, stirring, 10 minutes. Add puree and basil, boil, uncovered, about 15 minutes or until slightly thickened.

Cover base of shallow ovenproof dish (3 litre/12 cup capacity) with vegetable mixture, top with rice, then eggplant. Spread topping over eggplant, sprinkle with mozzarella. Bake, uncovered, in moderate oven about 45 minutes or until golden brown.

Topping: Combine all ingredients in bowl; mix well.

Serves 6 to 8.

■ Recipe can be made a day ahead.
■ Storage: Covered, in refrigerator.
■ Freeze: Cooked rice suitable.
■ Microwave: Rice suitable.

ABOVE: Cheesy Rice, Pepper and Eggplant Casserole.

PORK PARCELS WITH RICE, BACON AND BEANS

4 (600g) pork steaks
2 teaspoons vegetable oil
2 teaspoons cornflour
½ cup (125ml) dry white wine
1½ cups (375ml) chicken stock
3 teaspoons French mustard
3 teaspoons Worcestershire sauce
1 tablespoon chopped fresh parsley

FILLING
1 teaspoon vegetable oil
1 small (100g) red Spanish onion, chopped
2 bacon rashers, chopped
1 small (130g) apple, peeled, chopped
1 clove garlic, crushed
1½ cups cooked basmati rice
⅓ cup (70g) canned butter beans, rinsed, drained
3 teaspoons chopped fresh oregano

Place pork on board, top half of each steak with filling. Fold steaks over filling, secure with toothpicks. Heat oil in large pan, add pork, cook until lightly browned. Stir in blended cornflour and wine, then stock, mustard and sauce, simmer, uncovered, about 15 minutes or until pork is tender and sauce has thickened slightly. Remove pork from pan, keep warm. Simmer sauce, uncovered, until reduced by half; strain, stir in parsley. Serve pork parcels with sauce.

Filling: Heat oil in pan, add onion, bacon, apple and garlic, cook, stirring, until onion and apple are soft. Stir in remaining ingredients.

Serves 4.

■ Recipe can be prepared a day ahead.
■ Storage: Covered, in refrigerator.
■ Freeze: Suitable.
■ Microwave: Rice and filling suitable.

ABOVE: Pork Parcels with Rice, Bacon and Beans.

Tiles from Country Floors.

VEAL AND BACON ROLLS

**1½ cups cooked white
    short-grain rice**
300g minced veal
2 teaspoons olive oil
1 large (200g) onion, chopped
1 clove garlic, crushed
4 bacon rashers, chopped
1 tablespoon chopped fresh parsley
⅓ cup (25g) grated parmesan cheese
1 egg, lightly beaten
12 medium (960g) silverbeet leaves

TOMATO SAUCE
1 tablespoon olive oil
1 clove garlic, crushed
1 small (80g) onion, chopped
2 x 425g cans tomatoes
2 teaspoons sugar
1 tablespoon chopped fresh basil

Combine rice and veal in bowl. Heat oil in pan, add onion, garlic and bacon, cook, stirring, until onion is soft. Add onion mixture, parsley, cheese and egg to rice mixture; mix well.

Trim stalks from silverbeet, plunge leaves into boiling water 1 minute; drain immediately, rinse under cold water. Gently squeeze leaves to remove excess liquid; pat dry on absorbent paper.

Divide rice mixture into 12 portions, tightly wrap each portion in a silverbeet leaf, tucking in ends to enclose filling. Place rolls, seam side down, in ovenproof dish (3 litre/12 cup capacity), add tomato sauce. Bake, covered, in moderate oven about 45 minutes or until rolls are cooked.

Tomato Sauce: Heat oil in pan, add garlic and onion, cook, stirring, until onion is soft. Add undrained crushed tomatoes, sugar and basil, cook, uncovered, about 40 minutes or until slightly thickened.

Serves 6.

- Rolls can be made a day ahead.
- Storage: Covered, in refrigerator.
- Freeze: Cooked rice suitable.
- Microwave: Suitable.

ABOVE: Veal and Bacon Rolls.

BAKED RISOTTO WITH EGGPLANTS

2 medium (600g) eggplants
coarse cooking salt
2 tablespoons olive oil
2 medium (400g) red peppers
200g mozzarella cheese
1 cup (70g) stale breadcrumbs
2 tablespoons chopped fresh parsley

RISOTTO
1 litre (4 cups) beef stock
½ cup (125ml) dry white wine
1 tablespoon olive oil
2 cloves garlic, crushed
1 large (200g) onion, chopped
1 cup (200g) arborio rice
⅓ cup (25g) grated parmesan cheese

Cut eggplants into 5mm slices, place on wire rack, sprinkle with salt, stand 30 minutes. Rinse slices under cold water; drain, pat dry with absorbent paper. Place slices on oven tray, brush slices with oil, grill until lightly browned on both sides.

Quarter peppers, remove seeds and membranes. Grill peppers, skin side up, until skin blisters and blackens. Peel away skin, cut peppers into strips. Cut mozzarella into 1cm cubes.

Grease ovenproof dish (1.75 litre/7 cup capacity). Layer half the eggplants, half the risotto, half the cheese and half the peppers in prepared dish, repeat with remaining eggplants, risotto, cheese and peppers, top with combined crumbs and parsley. Bake, uncovered, in moderately hot oven about 25 minutes or until brown.
Risotto: Heat stock and wine in small pan, bring to boil; keep hot. Heat oil in large pan, add garlic and onion, cook, stirring, until onion is soft. Add rice, stir until combined. Stir ⅔ cup (160ml) hot stock into rice mixture, cook, stirring, over low heat until liquid is absorbed. Continue adding stock gradually, stirring until absorbed before next addition. Total cooking time should be about 35 minutes or until rice is tender. Stir in cheese.

Serves 4 to 6.

- Recipe can be prepared a day ahead.
- Storage: Covered, in refrigerator.
- Freeze: Not suitable.
- Microwave: Risotto suitable.

BELOW: Baked Risotto with Eggplants.

Serviette and basket from Barbara's Storehouse.

VEAL CUTLETS WITH SAGE RICE AND PROSCIUTTO

8 slices (120g) prosciutto
8 (1kg) veal cutlets
2 teaspoons olive oil
½ cup (125ml) beef stock
½ cup (125ml) tomato puree
¼ cup (60ml) dry white wine
1 teaspoon sugar

SAGE RICE
⅔ cup cooked brown rice and
    wild rice blend
¼ cup (35g) chopped pistachios,
    toasted
2 tablespoons grated parmesan
    cheese
2 tablespoons chopped fresh chives
3 teaspoons chopped fresh sage
1 egg, lightly beaten

Cut prosciutto slices into 3 strips lengthways. Secure tail end of cutlets with toothpicks. Heat oil in pan, add cutlets, cook until cutlets are well browned on both sides; remove from pan.

Top cutlets with sage rice, wrap 3 strips of prosciutto firmly around each cutlet. Return cutlets to pan, add stock, puree, wine and sugar, simmer, covered, about 20 minutes or until cutlets are tender and sauce slightly thickened. Remove cutlets from pan; strain sauce. Discard toothpicks. Serve veal with sauce.

Sage Rice: Combine all ingredients in bowl; mix well.

Serves 4.

■ Recipe can be prepared a day ahead.
■ Storage: Covered, in refrigerator.
■ Freeze: Suitable.
■ Microwave: Rice suitable.

VEAL AND RICE BALLS IN TOMATO SAUCE

1 cup (200g) white short-grain rice
750g minced veal
3 green shallots, finely chopped
2 cloves garlic, crushed
½ teaspoon ground cumin
¼ teaspoon dry mustard
¼ teaspoon ground cinnamon
1 tablespoon chopped fresh parsley
1 tablespoon chopped fresh
    coriander
½ teaspoon grated fresh ginger
1 egg, lightly beaten

TOMATO SAUCE
2 teaspoons olive oil
1 clove garlic, crushed
1 large (200g) onion, chopped
1 teaspoon grated fresh ginger
4 x 425g cans tomatoes
1 tablespoon sugar

Place rice in bowl, cover with cold water, cover, stand overnight. Drain rice, spread out to dry on clean tea-towel.

Combine veal with remaining ingredients in bowl; mix well. Roll level

58

tablespoons of mixture into balls, roll in dried rice. Steam in Chinese steamer about 20 minutes or until tender. Serve hot with tomato sauce.

Tomato Sauce: Heat oil in pan, add garlic, onion and ginger, cook, stirring, until onion is soft. Add undrained crushed tomatoes and sugar, simmer, uncovered, about 45 minutes or until thickened.

Serves 6.

- ■ Veal and rice balls best made just before serving. Sauce can be made a day ahead.
- ■ Storage: Covered, in refrigerator.
- ■ Freeze: Not suitable.
- ■ Microwave: Not suitable.

LEFT: Veal Cutlets with Sage Rice and Prosciutto.
ABOVE: From left: Veal and Rice Balls in Tomato Sauce, Parmesan Risotto with Veal and Olive Ragout.

Left: Plates and cutlery from Basic Essentials.
Above: Setting from Accoutrement.

PARMESAN RISOTTO WITH VEAL AND OLIVE RAGOUT

1kg diced veal
plain flour
¼ cup (60ml) olive oil
1 large (200g) onion, sliced
300g button mushrooms
2 cloves garlic, crushed
1 cup (250ml) dry white wine
2 x 425g cans tomatoes
1 cup (250ml) beef stock
1 teaspoon dried oregano leaves
2 bay leaves
1 teaspoon sugar
½ cup (80g) seedless green olives

PARMESAN RISOTTO
3 cups (750ml) chicken stock
60g butter
1 small (80g) onion, finely chopped
1 clove garlic, crushed
1 cup (200g) arborio rice
pinch saffron threads
⅓ cup (25g) grated parmesan cheese

Dust veal with flour, shake away excess flour. Heat half the oil in pan, add veal in batches, cook until well browned; remove from pan. Heat remaining oil in same pan, add onion, mushrooms and garlic, cook, stirring, until onion is soft. Add wine, cook, stirring, 1 minute.

Return veal to pan, add undrained crushed tomatoes, stock, oregano, bay leaves and sugar, simmer, uncovered, about 1 hour or until veal is tender. Stir in olives. Serve with parmesan risotto.

Parmesan Risotto: Heat stock in small pan, bring to boil; keep hot. Heat half the butter in large pan, add onion and garlic, cook, stirring, until onion is soft. Add rice and saffron, stir until combined. Stir ⅔ cup (160ml) hot stock mixture into rice mixture, cook, stirring, over low heat until liquid is absorbed. Continue adding stock gradually, stirring until absorbed before next addition. Cooking time should be about 35 minutes or until rice is tender. Stir in cheese and remaining butter.

Serves 4.

- ■ Veal can be made a day ahead. Risotto best made just before serving.
- ■ Storage: Veal, covered, in refrigerator.
- ■ Freeze: Not suitable.
- ■ Microwave: Risotto suitable.

NEAPOLITAN RICE CAKE

1½ cups (105g) stale breadcrumbs
350g minced beef
2 cloves garlic, crushed
¼ cup (20g) grated romano cheese
1 egg, lightly beaten
2 tablespoons chopped fresh parsley
2 tablespoons olive oil
3 (200g) Italian sausages
1 medium (150g) onion, sliced
150g button mushrooms, sliced
1 medium (200g) yellow pepper,
chopped
425g can tomatoes
250g mozzarella cheese, chopped

RICE SHELL
6 cups cooked arborio rice
50g butter, melted
1 egg, lightly beaten
⅓ cup (25g) grated romano cheese

Grease deep 22cm round cake pan, cover base with baking paper. Sprinkle base and side with some of the breadcrumbs. Combine beef, remaining breadcrumbs, garlic, romano cheese, egg and parsley in bowl; mix well. Roll level tablespoons of mixture into balls.

Heat oil in pan, add meatballs in batches, cook until well browned; drain on absorbent paper. Add sausages to same pan, cook until browned; slice sausages. Add onion, mushrooms and pepper to same pan, cook, stirring, 5 minutes. Add undrained crushed tomatoes, cook, stirring, until thickened. Stir in meatballs, sausages and mozzarella.

Press 3 cups of rice mixture firmly over base and side of prepared pan, fill carefully with meatball mixture, top with remaining rice; press firmly. Bake, uncovered, in moderate oven 40 minutes.

Rice Shell: Combine all ingredients in bowl; mix well.

Serves 6 to 8.

- ◼ Filling and rice can be prepared a day ahead. Recipe can be assembled several hours ahead.
- ◼ Storage: Covered, separately, in refrigerator.
- ◼ Freeze: Not suitable.
- ◼ Microwave: Rice suitable.

ABOVE: Neapolitan Rice Cake.

Red tray from Morris Home & Garden Wares.

ROASTED VEGETABLES WITH HARISSA RICE SALAD

1 large (350g) red pepper,
   thickly sliced
2 large (360g) carrots, thickly sliced
3 medium (360g) zucchini,
   thickly sliced
2 fresh corn cobs, quartered
6 baby (150g) onions, halved
1 teaspoon cumin seeds
1 tablespoon olive oil

HARISSA RICE SALAD
1 large (350g) red pepper
1 teaspoon ground cumin
1 teaspoon ground coriander
1 tablespoon lime juice
2 cloves garlic, crushed
3 small fresh red chillies, seeded,
   chopped
¼ cup (60ml) olive oil
2 tablespoons chopped fresh mint
3 cups cooked basmati rice

Combine vegetables, seeds and oil in baking dish; mix well. Bake, uncovered, in hot oven about 50 minutes or until vegetables are tender, stirring occasionally. Serve vegetables with harissa rice salad.

Harissa Rice Salad: Quarter pepper, remove seeds and membranes. Grill pepper, skin side up, until skin blisters and blackens. Peel away skin, chop pepper roughly. Blend or process pepper, spices, juice, garlic and chillies until smooth. Transfer mixture to large bowl, whisk in oil, stir in mint and rice.

Serves 4.

■ Harissa rice salad can be made
   a day ahead.
■ Storage: Covered, in refrigerator.
■ Freeze: Cooked rice suitable.
■ Microwave: Rice suitable.

BELOW: Roasted Vegetables with Harissa Rice Salad.

Setting from Accoutrement.

PORK BIRIANI

1 tablespoon vegetable oil
1 large (200g) onion, finely sliced
1 tablespoon grated fresh ginger
1 teaspoon cumin seeds
3 teaspoons vindaloo curry paste
600g pork fillet, finely sliced
425g can tomatoes
½ cup (125ml) tomato paste
½ cup (125ml) water
½ cup (125ml) sour cream

COCONUT RICE
100g ghee
2 large (400g) onions, finely sliced
2 cloves garlic, crushed
2 teaspoons yellow mustard seeds
1 cinnamon stick
6 cardamom pods, crushed
2 teaspoons ground turmeric
2 cups (400g) basmati rice
1 cup (70g) shredded coconut,
   toasted
2 x 400ml cans coconut cream
1 cup (250ml) water

Heat oil in pan, add onion, ginger, seeds and curry paste, cook, stirring, until onion is soft. Add pork, cook, stirring, until lightly browned. Add undrained crushed tomatoes, tomato paste and water, cook, stirring occasionally, until thickened slightly; stir in sour cream.

Spoon half the coconut rice into oven-proof dish (4 litre/16 cup capacity), top with pork curry, then remaining coconut rice. Bake, uncovered, in moderately hot oven about 20 minutes or until heated through. Serve sprinkled with flaked coconut, if desired.

Coconut Rice: Heat ghee in pan, add onions, garlic, seeds, cinnamon, cardamom and turmeric, cook, stirring, over heat until onions are soft. Stir in rice, coconut, coconut cream and water. Bring to boil, simmer, covered tightly, about 15 minutes or until most of the liquid is absorbed. Remove from heat, stand, covered, 10 minutes. Discard cinnamon and cardamom. Fluff rice with a fork.

Serves 6 to 8.
- Recipe can be made a day ahead.
- Storage: Covered, in refrigerator.
- Freeze: Not suitable.
- Microwave: Not suitable.

BELOW: Pork Biriani.

Black bowl from Orson & Blake.

CURRIED RICE PATTIES AND VEGETABLE STACK

2 medium (600g) eggplants
coarse cooking salt
1 large (350g) red pepper
8 x 8cm pappadums with pepper
vegetable oil for deep-frying

CURRIED RICE PATTIES
½ cup (100g) brown lentils
2 teaspoons vegetable oil
1 small (80g) onion, finely chopped
1 clove garlic, crushed
½ cup (100g) jasmine rice
1 tablespoon green curry paste
½ teaspoon cumin seeds
½ teaspoon ground turmeric
½ cup (125ml) dry white wine
425ml can coconut milk
1 cup (250ml) water
1 tablespoon chopped fresh
**   coriander**
¼ cup (40g) polenta

CUCUMBER YOGURT
1 small (130g) green cucumber,
**   seeded, finely chopped**
1 cup (250ml) plain yogurt
1 tablespoon chopped fresh
**   coriander**

Cut eggplants into 1cm slices, place in colander, sprinkle with salt, stand 30 minutes. Rinse under cold water; drain, pat dry. Quarter pepper, remove seeds and membranes. Grill pepper, skin side up, until skin blisters and blackens. Peel away skin, slice pepper.

Just before serving, deep-fry pappadums, eggplant and patties separately in batches in hot oil until browned; drain on absorbent paper. Serve patties, eggplant, pepper and yogurt cream between pappadums.

Curried Rice Patties: Add lentils to pan of boiling water, boil, uncovered, about 15 minutes or until tender; drain.

Heat oil in pan, add onion and garlic, cook, stirring, until onion is soft. Add rice, paste, seeds and turmeric, cook, stirring, until fragrant. Add wine, simmer, uncovered, until almost absorbed. Stir in coconut milk and water, simmer, uncovered, about 15 minutes or until rice is tender. Stir in coriander and lentils; cool.

Process half the mixture until smooth. Combine with remaining rice mixture. Shape level tablespoons of mixture into patties, coat in polenta; refrigerate until firm.

Cucumber Yogurt: Combine all ingredients in bowl; mix well.

Serves 6.

■ Patties and yogurt cream can be prepared a day ahead.
■ Storage: Covered, separately, in refrigerator.
■ Freeze: Not suitable.
■ Microwave: Pappadums and lentils suitable.

ABOVE: Curried Rice Patties and Vegetable Stack.

RICE NICOISE SALAD

2 (550g) tuna steaks
¾ cup (180ml) olive oil
½ cup (125ml) red wine vinegar
2 teaspoons chopped fresh parsley
2 teaspoons chopped fresh oregano
1 teaspoon chopped fresh basil
250g green beans, halved
1 large (200g) onion, chopped
2 cloves garlic, crushed
1 medium (200g) red pepper, sliced
1 cup (120g) seedless black olives
6 cups cooked white long-grain rice
¼ cup (60ml) cider vinegar

Cut tuna into 2cm pieces. Combine tuna, 2 tablespoons of the oil, red wine vinegar and herbs in bowl; refrigerate 30 minutes.

Boil, steam or microwave beans until just tender; drain. Heat 1 tablespoon of the remaining oil in pan, add drained tuna, onion and half the garlic, cook, stirring, until tuna and onion are tender. Remove from heat, combine tuna mixture with beans, pepper, olives and rice. Combine remaining oil, remaining garlic and cider vinegar in jar. Pour dressing over tuna mixture just before serving.

Serves 4 to 6.

■ Recipe can be prepared 3 hours ahead.
■ Storage: Covered, in refrigerator.
■ Freeze: Cooked rice suitable.
■ Microwave: Rice suitable.

SPICY PRAWN AND CHICKEN PATTIES

1½ cups cooked white short-grain rice
250g minced chicken
150g small cooked prawns, shelled
5 green shallots, chopped
2 cloves garlic, crushed
2 teaspoons grated fresh ginger
1 small fresh red chilli, chopped
1 tablespoon fish sauce
2 tablespoons chopped fresh coriander
vegetable oil for shallow-frying

YOGURT DIPPING SAUCE
1 cup (250ml) plain yogurt
1½ tablespoons mild sweet chilli sauce
1 green shallot, finely chopped
1 tablespoon chopped fresh coriander

Process rice, chicken, prawns, shallots, garlic, ginger, chilli, sauce and coriander until just combined. Divide mixture into 8 portions, shape into patties, place on tray, refrigerate 1 hour. Shallow-fry patties in hot oil until browned and cooked through; drain on absorbent paper.
Yogurt Dipping Sauce: Combine all ingredients in bowl; mix well.

Makes 8.

■ Recipe can be prepared a day ahead.
■ Storage: Covered, separately, in refrigerator.
■ Freeze: Patties suitable.
■ Microwave: Rice suitable.

CANTONESE-STYLE DEEP-FRIED CHICKEN

750g chicken breast fillets
1 tablespoon teriyaki sauce
1 tablespoon mild sweet chilli sauce
2 cloves garlic, crushed
2 teaspoons grated fresh ginger
¼ teaspoon five spice powder
1 egg, lightly beaten
½ cup (75g) rice flour
vegetable oil for deep-frying

CHILLI RICE
4 cups cooked jasmine rice
4 green shallots, finely chopped
1 small (130g) green cucumber, finely chopped
2 tablespoons mild sweet chilli sauce

Cut chicken into 3cm strips. Combine chicken, sauces, garlic, ginger and five spice powder in bowl; mix well. Cover, refrigerate overnight.

Add egg to chicken mixture, stir in flour. Deep-fry chicken in hot oil until browned and tender. Do not have oil too hot or

chicken will over-brown before cooking through. Serve with chilli rice.

Chilli Rice: Combine all ingredients in bowl; mix well.

Serves 4

■ Recipe can be prepared a day ahead.
■ Storage: Covered, separately, in refrigerator.
■ Freeze: Not suitable.
■ Microwave: Rice suitable.

LEFT: From back: Spicy Prawn and Chicken Patties, Rice Niçoise Salad.
ABOVE: From left: Chicken and Bacon Fried Rice, Cantonese-Style Deep-Fried Chicken.

Left: Setting from Pacific East India Company.

CHICKEN AND BACON FRIED RICE

500g chicken thigh fillets, chopped
1 clove garlic, crushed
2 teaspoons grated fresh ginger
2 tablespoons rice vinegar
4½ cups cooked white long-grain rice
1 tablespoon peanut oil
3 bacon rashers, chopped
2 tablespoons soy sauce
1 tablespoon rice vinegar, extra

Combine chicken, garlic, ginger and vinegar in bowl; mix well. Cover, refrigerate several hours or overnight. Spread rice on a tray, cover with absorbent paper; refrigerate overnight.

Heat oil in wok or large pan, add bacon, stir-fry until crisp; drain on absorbent paper. Add chicken to wok in batches, stir-fry until tender. Return chicken, bacon, rice, sauce and extra vinegar to wok, stir-fry until heated through.

Serves 4.

■ Recipe can be prepared a day ahead.
■ Storage: Covered, separately, in refrigerator.
■ Freeze: Cooked rice suitable.
■ Microwave: Rice suitable.

SPANISH-STYLE RICE WITH POTATOES AND ONIONS

250g medium uncooked prawns
250g calamari hoods
1 tablespoon olive oil
6 baby (150g) brown onions
18 baby (720g) new potatoes, halved
2 cups (400g) white short-grain rice
2 cloves garlic, crushed
2 teaspoons paprika
¼ teaspoon saffron powder
1.25 litres (5 cups) chicken stock
425g can tomatoes
500g firm white fish fillets, chopped

Shell and devein prawns, leaving tails intact. Cut shallow diagonal slashes in criss-cross pattern on inside surface of calamari; cut calamari into rectangles.

Heat oil in large heavy-based pan, add onions and potatoes, cook, stirring, 5 minutes or until onions are lightly browned and just beginning to soften. Add rice, garlic, paprika and saffron, cook, stirring, 2 minutes. Add 1 litre (4 cups) of the boiling stock and undrained crushed tomatoes, simmer, covered, for 12 minutes. Add seafood and remaining boiling stock, simmer, covered, until seafood and rice are tender and most of the liquid absorbed.

Serves 4 to 6.

- ■ Recipe best made just before serving.
- ■ Freeze: Not suitable.
- ■ Microwave: Suitable.

PRAWN RISOTTO

800g medium uncooked prawns
2 tablespoons vegetable oil
50g butter
3 green shallots, chopped
2 cloves garlic, crushed
200g button mushrooms, sliced
2½ cups (500g) arborio rice
3 cups (750ml) water
3 cups (750ml) vegetable stock
½ cup (125ml) dry white wine
1 tablespoon chopped fresh parsley
1 teaspoon cracked black pepper
1 tablespoon chopped fresh chives
¼ cup (20g) grated parmesan cheese

Shell and devein prawns, leaving tails intact. Heat oil and butter in pan, add shallots, garlic and mushrooms, cook, stirring, until shallots are soft, stir in rice. Combine water, stock and wine in another pan, bring to boil, keep hot.

Stir ⅔ cup (160ml) hot stock mixture into rice mixture, cook, stirring, over low heat until liquid is absorbed. Continue adding stock mixture gradually, stirring until absorbed before next addition. Total cooking time should be about 35 minutes or until rice is tender. Stir in prawns, simmer, covered, until prawns are tender. Stir in remaining ingredients.

Serves 4 to 6.

- ■ Recipe best made just before serving.
- ■ Freeze: Not suitable.
- ■ Microwave: Suitable.

SEASONED BAKED SQUID

500g small mussels
1 tablespoon olive oil
1 clove garlic, crushed
1 small (200g) leek, chopped
400g scallops, chopped
500g uncooked prawns, shelled
1½ cups cooked white long-grain rice
2 eggs, lightly beaten
24 small (950g) squid hoods

TOMATO SAUCE
¼ cup (60ml) olive oil
1 large (200g) onion, chopped
2 cloves garlic, crushed
4 x 425g cans tomatoes
1 tablespoon sugar
1 tablespoon shredded fresh basil

Scrub mussels, remove beards. Boil, steam or microwave mussels until shells open. Remove mussels from shells. Heat oil in pan, add garlic and leek, cook, stirring, until leek is soft. Add scallops and chopped prawns, cook, stirring, 3 minutes; drain. Add mussels; cool. Combine seafood mixture with rice and eggs; spoon into squid hoods, secure with toothpicks. Place squid in ovenproof dish, add tomato sauce, bake, covered, in moderate oven about 30 minutes or until tender.

Tomato Sauce: Heat oil in large pan, add onion and garlic, cook, stirring, until onion is soft. Add undrained crushed tomatoes, sugar and basil, simmer, uncovered, about 45 minutes or until slightly thickened.

Serves 6.

- ■ Recipe best made close to serving.
- ■ Freeze: Cooked rice suitable.
- ■ Microwave: Rice suitable.

FISH IN BEER BATTER WITH TARRAGON MAYONNAISE

1 cup (150g) rice flour
⅓ cup (50g) self-raising flour
1⅓ cups (330ml) beer
1 tablespoon chopped fresh chives
6 firm white fish fillets
plain flour
vegetable oil for shallow-frying

TARRAGON MAYONNAISE
1 cup (250ml) mayonnaise
2 teaspoons chopped fresh tarragon
1 green shallot, finely chopped
1 teaspoon drained capers, finely chopped
1 teaspoon lemon juice

Sift rice and self-raising flours together in medium bowl, gradually stir in beer, then chives. Toss fish in plain flour, shake away excess flour. Dip fish into beer batter, shallow-fry fish in hot oil until golden brown and cooked through; drain on absorbent paper. Serve with tarragon mayonnaise.
Tarragon Mayonnaise: Combine all ingredients in small bowl; mix well.

Serves 6.

- ■ Recipe best made close to serving.
- ■ Freeze: Not suitable.
- ■ Microwave: Not suitable.

LEFT: From back: Prawn Risotto, Spanish-Style Rice with Potatoes and Onions.
BELOW: From left: Fish in Beer Batter with Tarragon Mayonnaise, Seasoned Baked Squid.

Left: Setting from Morris Home & Garden Wares.
Below: Setting from Barbara's Storehouse.

PUMPKIN RICE

You will need about 600g butternut pumpkin for this recipe.

1½ cups (300g) white short-grain rice
4 cups grated uncooked butternut pumpkin
1 tablespoon chopped fresh coriander
¼ teaspoon ground nutmeg
425ml can coconut milk
½ cup (125ml) milk
30g butter, chopped
2 tablespoons pumpkin seed kernels
2 tablespoons sunflower seed kernels

Soak rice in bowl of cold water 2 hours; drain. Combine rice, pumpkin, coriander and nutmeg in bowl; mix well. Place mixture in greased deep ovenproof dish (1.5 litre/6 cup capacity), pour over combined milks. Dot with butter, sprinkle with combined seeds. Bake, uncovered, in moderate oven about 45 minutes or until rice is tender and liquid absorbed.

Serves 4.

■ Recipe best made close to serving.
■ Freeze: Not suitable.
■ Microwave: Not suitable.

ABOVE: Pumpkin Rice.
RIGHT: Creole-Style Beef with Avocado Salsa.

Right: Setting from The Bay Tree Kitchen Shop.

CREOLE-STYLE BEEF WITH AVOCADO SALSA

2 tablespoons olive oil
750g beef rump steak, finely chopped
2 medium (300g) onions,
   finely chopped
35g packet taco seasoning mix
425g can tomatoes
1 cup (250ml) dry red wine
2 cups (500ml) water
¼ cup (50g) basmati rice
340g packet flour tortillas
¾ cup (180ml) sour cream

AVOCADO SALSA
1 small (150g) red pepper
1 medium (250g) avocado, mashed
1 medium (130g) tomato,
   finely chopped
1 small (100g) red Spanish onion,
   finely chopped
1 clove garlic, crushed
1 tablespoon lemon juice

Heat half the oil in pan, add beef in batches, cook, stirring, until browned, remove from pan. Heat remaining oil in same pan, add onions, cook, stirring, until onions are soft. Stir in seasoning mix, undrained crushed tomatoes, wine and water. Return beef to pan, simmer, covered, about 35 minutes or until beef is tender. Stir in rice, simmer 15 minutes or until rice is tender. Serve warmed tortillas topped with beef mixture, avocado salsa and sour cream.

Avocado Salsa: Quarter pepper, remove seeds and membranes. Grill pepper, skin side up, until skin blisters and blackens. Peel away skin, chop pepper finely. Combine all ingredients in bowl; mix well.

Serves 4 to 6.

- Beef mixture can be prepared a day ahead. Avocado salsa best made just before serving.
- Storage: Covered, in refrigerator.
- Freeze: Not suitable.
- Microwave: Not suitable.

SWEET 'N' SPICY JAMAICAN CHICKEN

**4 single (1kg) chicken breasts
   on the bone
2 teaspoons sambal oelek
2 medium (300g) onions, quartered
1 tablespoon grated fresh ginger
1 teaspoon ground allspice
2 cloves garlic, crushed
¼ cup (60ml) salt-reduced soy sauce
¼ cup (50g) brown sugar
1 tablespoon lime juice
1 bunch (120g) rocket**

FILLING

**1 tablespoon olive oil
1 medium (150g) onion, chopped
1 clove garlic, crushed
1 teaspoon paprika
1 cup cooked white long-grain rice
¼ cup chopped fresh parsley
2 tablespoons chopped roasted
   unsalted cashews**

PINEAPPLE SALSA

**6 medium (450g) egg tomatoes
salt, pepper
1 teaspoon sugar
450g can pineapple pieces in
   syrup, drained**

Remove chicken meat from bones; discard bones. Process sambal oelek, onions, ginger, allspice, garlic, sauce, sugar and juice until smooth. Combine chicken with onion mixture in shallow baking dish, cover, refrigerate 1 hour.

Remove chicken from onion mixture, loosen skin on 1 side of each breast by sliding a finger carefully between skin and meat; spread a quarter of the filling under the skin of each breast. Return chicken to baking dish, bake, uncovered, in hot oven about 20 minutes or until chicken is tender, brushing occasionally with onion mixture. Remove chicken from dish, grill, skin side up, until skin is crisp. Reserve onion mixture for pineapple salsa. Serve chicken on rocket leaves with pineapple salsa.

Filling: Heat oil in small pan, add onion, garlic and paprika, cook, stirring, until onion is soft. Process onion mixture, rice, parsley and nuts until roughly chopped.

Pineapple Salsa: Halve tomatoes lengthways, place, cut side up, on oven tray, sprinkle with salt, pepper and sugar. Bake, uncovered, in very hot oven about 20 minutes or until tomatoes blacken slightly around the edges; cool. Process tomatoes, pineapple and reserved onion mixture until chopped.

Serves 4.

■ Filling can be made a day ahead.
■ Storage: Covered, in refrigerator.
■ Freeze: Cooked rice suitable.
■ Microwave: Filling suitable.

QUAIL AND MUSHROOM PAELLA

4 (680g) quail
1 double (350g) chicken breast fillet
2 small fresh red chillies,
    finely chopped
2 cloves garlic, crushed
2 tablespoons lemon juice
¼ cup (60ml) olive oil
1 medium (150g) onion, sliced
250g button mushrooms
100g shitake mushrooms
1 small (150g) red pepper, sliced
1 small (150g) green pepper, sliced
2 cups (400g) white long-grain rice
1.25 litres (5 cups) chicken stock
pinch saffron threads
¾ cup (90g) frozen peas, thawed
2 medium (260g) tomatoes, peeled,
    seeded, chopped
2 tablespoons chopped fresh parsley

Cut each quail into 4 pieces. Cut chicken fillet into 6 pieces. Combine quail, chicken, chillies, garlic and juice in bowl. Cover, refrigerate 3 hours or overnight.

Heat oil in pan, add quail and chicken in batches, cook until browned and tender, remove from pan; keep warm. Drain all but 2 tablespoons of oil from pan, add onion, mushrooms and peppers, cook, stirring, until vegetables are soft. Stir in rice, stock and saffron, simmer, uncovered, about 10 minutes or until most of the liquid is absorbed. Add peas and tomatoes, cook few minutes or until rice is tender. Return chicken and quail to pan, serve sprinkled with parsley.

Serves 4.

- ■ Recipe best made just before serving.
- ■ Freeze: Not suitable.
- ■ Microwave: Not suitable.

CHILLI CRAB AND PRAWN COMBINATION RICE

1kg uncooked mud crab
1kg uncooked king prawns
2 tablespoons peanut oil
1 medium (200g) red pepper, sliced
2 medium (300g) onions, sliced
4 cloves garlic, crushed
1 teaspoon grated fresh ginger
1 teaspoon grated lime rind
⅓ cup (80ml) mild sweet chilli sauce
1 tablespoon fish sauce
2 tablespoons soy sauce
4 cups cooked jasmine rice
4 green shallots, chopped
¼ cup chopped fresh coriander
2 tablespoons lime juice

Place live crab in freezer for at least 2 hours; this is the most humane way of killing a crab.

Slide a sharp strong knife under top of shell at back of crab, lever off shell and discard. Remove and discard gills, wash crab thoroughly. Chop body into quarters with cleaver, remove legs and claws, chop claws into large pieces.

Shell and devein prawns, leaving tails intact. Heat oil in large pan, add pepper, onions, garlic, ginger, rind and sauces, cook, stirring, 2 minutes. Add crab, cook, covered, 5 minutes. Stir in prawns, cook, covered, 5 minutes or until seafood is cooked through. Stir in remaining ingredients, stir over heat until hot.

Serves 6.

- ■ Recipe best made just before serving.
- ■ Freeze: Not suitable.
- ■ Microwave: Rice suitable.

LEFT: From back: Quail and Mushroom Paella, Sweet 'n' Spicy Jamaican Chicken. ABOVE: Chilli Crab and Prawn Combination Rice.

*Left: Plates from Morris Home & Garden Wares.
Above: Bowl from House.*

CREAMY SEAFOOD RICE FLANS

4 cups cooked white short-grain rice
1 egg yolk
½ cup (60g) grated tasty cheddar cheese
1 tablespoon chopped fresh parsley

FILLING
1 tablespoon olive oil
250g firm white fish fillets
400g medium uncooked prawns, shelled
250g scallops
1 small (200g) leek, sliced
2 cloves garlic, crushed
¼ cup (60ml) dry white wine
300ml cream
2 teaspoons Dijon mustard
½ cup (60g) grated tasty cheddar cheese

Grease 4 shallow ovenproof dishes (1⅓ cup/330ml capacity). Combine rice, egg yolk and cheese in bowl; mix well. Press rice mixture over base and sides of prepared dishes. Spoon filling into rice cases. Bake in moderately hot oven about 20 minutes or until lightly browned. Serve sprinkled with parsley.

Filling: Heat half the oil in pan, add fish, cook until tender, remove from pan; chop into large pieces. Add prawns to same pan, cook, stirring, until tender, remove from pan. Add scallops, cook, stirring, until tender, remove from pan. Drain any liquid from seafood; reserve.

Heat remaining oil in same pan, add leek and garlic, cook, stirring, until leek is soft. Add wine and reserved liquid, simmer, uncovered, until liquid has evaporated. Add cream and mustard, simmer, uncovered, until thickened. Remove from heat, stir in cheese and seafood.

Makes 4.

- Rice cases can be made a day ahead. Filling best made on day of serving.
- Storage: Covered, in refrigerator.
- Freeze: Cooked rice suitable.
- Microwave: Rice suitable.

ABOVE: From back: Creamy Seafood Rice Flans, Thai Salmon and Rice Fillo Pastries.
RIGHT: Mediterranean-Style Beef.

Above: Checked plate from Waterford Wedgwood.
Right: China from Villeroy & Boch; tiles from Country Floors.

THAI SALMON AND RICE FILLO PASTRIES

2 teaspoons vegetable oil
12 (120g) French shallots, chopped
1 tablespoon mild curry paste
415g can salmon, drained, flaked
2 cups cooked jasmine rice
2 small (260g) green cucumbers, seeded, chopped
12 sheets fillo pastry
60g butter, melted
2 tablespoons dried onion flakes

TOMATO LEMON GRASS SAUCE
1 tablespoon vegetable oil
1 small fresh red chilli, chopped
1 small (80g) onion, chopped
1 clove garlic, crushed
2cm piece fresh ginger
2 x 425g cans tomatoes
2 stems fresh lemon grass, bruised
2 teaspoons tomato paste
1 teaspoon brown sugar

Heat oil in pan, add shallots and curry paste, cook, stirring, until fragrant. Combine shallot mixture, salmon, rice and cucumbers in bowl.

Cut pastry sheets in half lengthways. Layer 2 pastry strips, brushing each with butter. Divide salmon mixture into 12 portions. Place 1 portion on the diagonal at 1 end of layered pastry. Fold to form a triangle, continue folding to end of strip, retaining triangular shape. Brush triangle with a little more butter. Repeat with remaining pastry, butter and filling.

Place triangles on greased oven tray, bake in moderate oven 15 minutes, sprinkle with onion flakes, bake 5 minutes. Serve with tomato lemon grass sauce.

Tomato Lemon Grass Sauce: Heat oil in pan, add chilli, onion, garlic and ginger, stir until onion is soft. Add undrained crushed tomatoes, lemon grass, paste and sugar, simmer, uncovered, about 45 minutes or until mixture thickens, stirring occasionally. Discard lemon grass and ginger. Blend or process mixture until smooth, strain. Return sauce to pan, stir until hot.

Serves 6.

- Sauce can be made 2 days ahead.
- Storage: Covered, in refrigerator.
- Freeze: Cooked rice suitable.
- Microwave: Rice suitable.

MEDITERRANEAN-STYLE BEEF

1kg piece beef scotch fillet
1 tablespoon olive oil
1 small (100g) red Spanish onion, roughly chopped
2 small (180g) zucchini, sliced
1 clove garlic, crushed
1 medium (130g) tomato, peeled, chopped
3 teaspoons chopped fresh rosemary
½ cup cooked white long-grain rice
2 tablespoons sultanas
2 teaspoons olive oil, extra

Cut 5 deep diagonal slashes, two-thirds into the fillet, about 2cm apart. Place fillet in greased baking dish. Heat oil in pan, add onion, zucchini and garlic, cook, stirring, until onion is soft. Add tomato and rosemary, cook, stirring, until tomato is just soft. Stir in rice and sultanas.

Fill slashes in fillet with tomato mixture, brush with extra oil. Bake, uncovered, in moderate oven about 40 minutes or until cooked as desired.

Serves 4 to 6.

- Recipe can be prepared 3 hours ahead.
- Storage: Covered, in refrigerator.
- Freeze: Cooked rice suitable.
- Microwave: Rice suitable.

RICE MOUSSAKA

2 large (1kg) eggplants
coarse cooking salt
⅓ cup (80ml) olive oil
1 clove garlic, crushed
5 green shallots, chopped
200g button mushrooms, sliced
¼ cup (60ml) dry white wine
2 x 425g cans tomatoes
1 tablespoon tomato paste
1 teaspoon ground cinnamon
2 teaspoons sugar
¼ cup chopped fresh parsley
3 cups cooked white short-grain rice
⅓ cup (25g) grated parmesan cheese
½ teaspoon ground nutmeg

SAUCE
125g butter
⅔ cup (100g) plain flour
2¾ cups (680ml) milk
300ml cream
⅓ cup (25g) grated parmesan cheese
1 egg yolk

Cut eggplants into 5mm slices, place on wire rack, sprinkle with salt, stand 30 minutes. Rinse slices under cold water; drain, pat dry. Place slices in single layer on oven trays, brush with half the oil, grill on both sides until lightly browned; drain.

Heat remaining oil in pan, add garlic, shallots and mushrooms, cook, stirring, until shallots are soft. Add wine, cook, uncovered, until liquid has evaporated. Add undrained crushed tomatoes, paste, cinnamon, sugar and parsley, simmer, covered, about 30 minutes or until liquid is slightly thickened. Stir in rice and cheese.

Grease ovenproof dish (3 litre/12 cup capacity). Place one-third of the eggplant over base of dish, top with half the rice mixture, then half the remaining eggplant, all the remaining rice mixture and remaining eggplant. Spread sauce over eggplant, sprinkle with nutmeg. Bake, uncovered, in moderate oven about 30 minutes or until lightly browned.

Sauce: Melt butter in pan, stir in flour, stir over heat until bubbling. Remove from heat, gradually stir in milk and cream, stir over heat until mixture boils and thickens. Remove from heat, stir in cheese and yolk.

Serves 6 to 8.

- Recipe can be made a day ahead.
- Storage: Covered, in refrigerator.
- Freeze: Suitable.
- Microwave: Rice suitable.

BELOW: From back: Nutty Olive and Rice Meatloaf, Rice Moussaka.

NUTTY OLIVE AND RICE MEATLOAF

500g sausage mince
500g pork and veal mince
1 tablespoon chopped fresh parsley
1 egg, lightly beaten
¼ cup (60ml) olive oil

FILLING
2 cups cooked white short-grain rice
1 tablespoon chopped fresh parsley
2 teaspoons chopped fresh oregano
1 teaspoon grated lemon rind
¼ cup (40g) pine nuts
**2 tablespoons sliced seedless
    black olives**
1 clove garlic, crushed
4 green shallots, sliced
1 egg, lightly beaten

Combine both minces, parsley and egg in bowl; mix well. Press mixture firmly into 24cm x 28cm rectangle on greased foil. Spoon filling along longest edge, leaving 3cm border. Carefully roll mince over filling, pinch ends to seal. Add 2 tablespoons of the oil to baking dish, place meatloaf, seam side down, in dish, brush with remaining oil. Bake, uncovered, in moderate oven about 45 minutes or until cooked through.
Filling: Combine all ingredients in bowl; mix well.

Serves 6.

- Recipe can be prepared a day ahead.
- Storage: Covered, in refrigerator.
- Freeze: Cooked rice suitable
- Microwave: Rice suitable.

SAFFRON RICE GUMBO WITH SEAFOOD

300g medium uncooked prawns
300g firm white fish fillets
12 small (200g) mussels
150g okra
1 tablespoon olive oil
**1 medium (170g) red Spanish onion,
    chopped**
**1 medium (200g) red pepper,
    roughly chopped**
**2 small fresh red chillies,
    finely chopped**
2 cloves garlic, crushed
¾ cup (150g) arborio rice
1 teaspoon ground turmeric
pinch saffron powder
1.25 litres (5 cups) vegetable stock
¾ cup (180ml) dry white wine
130g can corn kernels, drained
1 tablespoon chopped fresh dill

Shell and devein prawns, leaving heads and tails intact. Cut fish into 5cm lengths. Scrub mussels, remove beards. Trim stems from okra. Heat oil in pan, add okra, onion, pepper, chillies and garlic, cook, stirring, until onion is soft. Add rice, turmeric and saffron, cook, stirring, 1 minute. Add stock and wine, simmer, uncovered, about 15 minutes or until rice is tender, stirring occasionally. Add prawns and fish, cook, stirring, about 3 minutes. Stir in mussels and corn, cook until mussels are tender. Stir in dill.

Serves 4 to 6.

- Recipe best made close to serving.
- Freeze: Not suitable.
- Microwave: Not suitable.

ABOVE: Saffron Rice Gumbo with Seafood.

Copper pot from The Bay Tree Kitchen Shop.

SPICY MINTED MEATBALLS

2 cloves garlic, crushed
3 bacon rashers, chopped
1 small (80g) onion, chopped
1 cup cooked basmati rice
500g minced beef
1 tablespoon soy sauce
2 teaspoons fish sauce
1 teaspoon garam masala
1 teaspoon ground cumin
1 tablespoon peanut oil
2 x 425g cans tomatoes
2 small fresh red chillies, chopped
¼ cup (35g) roasted unsalted
**   peanuts, chopped**
¾ cup (180ml) coconut milk
¼ cup chopped fresh mint

Add garlic, bacon and onion to pan, cook, stirring, until onion is soft, combine in bowl with rice, beef, sauces and spices. Shape level tablespoons of mixture into balls, place on tray, cover, refrigerate 30 minutes. Heat oil in large pan, add meatballs in batches, cook until browned. Return meatballs to pan, add undrained crushed tomatoes, chillies and peanuts, cook, stirring, until meatballs are cooked through. Stir in milk and mint, cook, stirring, until hot; do not boil. Serve with extra boiled rice sprinkled with parsley, if desired.

Serves 4.

- ▣ Recipe can be prepared a day ahead.
- ▣ Storage: Covered, in refrigerator.
- ▣ Freeze: Meatballs suitable.
- ▣ Microwave: Rice and onion mixture suitable.

BEEF AND RICE NOODLES

500g beef fillet, sliced
1 teaspoon sesame oil
2 cloves garlic, crushed
1 tablespoon grated fresh ginger
2 tablespoons mild sweet chilli sauce
1 tablespoon peanut oil
750g flat rice noodles
¼ cup (60ml) hoi sin sauce
¼ cup (60ml) water
¼ cup (35g) roasted unsalted
**   peanuts**

Combine beef, sesame oil, garlic, ginger and chilli sauce in bowl; cover, refrigerate 3 hours or overnight. Heat a little of the peanut oil in wok or pan, add beef in batches with remaining oil, stir-fry until beef is tender. Return beef to wok with noodles, hoi sin sauce and water, stir-fry gently until noodles are heated through, top with peanuts.

Serves 4.

- ▣ Beef best marinated a day ahead. Recipe best made just before serving.
- ▣ Storage: Covered, in refrigerator.
- ▣ Freeze: Not suitable.
- ▣ Microwave: Not suitable.

From left: Beef and Rice Noodles,
Spicy Minted Meatballs.

Setting from Pacific East India Company.

JAMBALAYA

6 (1kg) chicken thigh cutlets
1 teaspoon garlic salt
½ teaspoon cayenne pepper
1 teaspoon dried onion flakes
2 teaspoons vegetable oil
2 cloves garlic, crushed
**1 large (300g) red Spanish onion,
      chopped**
1 large (350g) red pepper, chopped
180g chorizo sausage
200g ham, chopped
2 bay leaves
1 sprig fresh thyme
3 cups (750ml) chicken stock
425g can tomatoes
2 cups (400g) white long-grain rice
2 green shallots, chopped
¼ cup chopped fresh parsley

Coat chicken with combined salt,
cayenne pepper and onion flakes. Heat oil
in pan, add chicken, cook until browned all
over; drain on absorbent paper.

Drain all but 1 tablespoon of oil from
pan. Add garlic, chopped onion, red
pepper, sausage and ham to pan, cook,
stirring, until onion is soft. Return chicken
to pan, stir in bay leaves, thyme and stock,
simmer, covered, 15 minutes. Add undrained crushed tomatoes and rice; mix
well. Simmer, covered, 15 minutes or until
most of the liquid has been absorbed and
rice is tender. Stir in shallots and parsley.

Serves 4 to 6.

■ Recipe best made just before serving.
■ Freeze: Not suitable.
■ Microwave: Not suitable.

ABOVE: Jambalaya.

Plate from House; setting from Accoutrement.

DUCK WITH WILD RICE AND ORANGE MUSTARD SAUCE

2 bacon rashers, chopped
1 small (80g) onion, finely chopped
300g can water chestnuts,
    drained, chopped
1/3 cup (55g) blanched almonds,
    toasted, chopped
1/4 cup chopped fresh chives
1/3 cup cooked wild rice
1/4 cup cooked white short-grain rice
8 (1.2kg) duck breast fillets
2 tablespoons olive oil

ORANGE MUSTARD SAUCE
1 1/2 cups (375ml) beef stock
2 cups (500ml) water
3 medium (540g) oranges,
    peeled, halved
2 tablespoons golden syrup
1 teaspoon seeded mustard
2 green shallots, finely chopped
1 teaspoon cornflour
1 tablespoon water, extra

Cook bacon and onion in pan, stirring, until onion is soft. Combine bacon mixture in bowl with chestnuts, almonds, chives and all the rice. Trim excess fat from duck. Cut a pocket in 1 side of each fillet; do not cut right through. Carefully push rice mixture into pockets; secure openings with toothpicks.

Heat oil in pan, cook fillets in batches, skin side down, until browned; turn and brown other side. Place fillets on wire rack in baking dish, bake, uncovered, in hot oven about 15 minutes or until tender. Serve with orange mustard sauce.

Orange Mustard Sauce: Heat stock, water and oranges in pan, boil, uncovered, 5 minutes, simmer, covered, 20 minutes; strain. Return liquid to pan, add golden syrup and mustard, boil, uncovered, 10 minutes. Add shallots and blended cornflour and extra water, stir until sauce boils and thickens.

Serves 4.

■ Seasoning can be made a day ahead.
■ Storage: Covered, in refrigerator.
■ Freeze: Seasoned fillets suitable.
■ Microwave: Rice suitable.

BELOW: Duck with Wild Rice and Orange Mustard Sauce.

China from Waterford Wedgwood; napery and coaster from Morris Home & Garden Wares; glass from H.A.G. Imports.

Accompaniments

There's a great cross-section of ideas here, with discoveries such as crispy rice chips (we couldn't stop eating them!), kumara and fennel risotto, and smoked cheese and rice pears. Easy, interesting rice salads will be very popular, and our versions of fried rice and nasi goreng are among the best ever. We've also made great-tasting basics, such as saffron rice, curry rice and herbed rice, so you need never be short of inspiration to satisfy every taste. Many recipes could easily double as scrumptious light meals. For helpful rice cooking tips, turn to page 120.

MUSHROOM AND SUN-DRIED TOMATO RISOTTO

1 litre (4 cups) chicken stock
2 cups (500ml) water
1 cup (250ml) dry white wine
2 tablespoons olive oil
30g butter
200g button mushrooms, sliced
200g flat mushrooms, sliced
1 medium (350g) leek, sliced
2 cloves garlic, crushed
2 cups (400g) arborio rice
½ cup (40g) grated parmesan cheese
⅓ cup (35g) drained sun-dried tomatoes, sliced
1 tablespoon chopped fresh oregano

Combine stock, water and wine in pan, bring to boil; keep hot. Heat oil and butter in another medium pan, add mushrooms, leek and garlic, cook, stirring, until leek is soft. Add rice, stir until combined. Stir ⅔ cup (160ml) hot stock mixture into rice mixture, cook, stirring, over low heat until liquid is absorbed.

Continue adding stock mixture gradually, stirring until absorbed before each addition. Total cooking time should be about 35 minutes or until rice is tender. Stir in cheese, tomatoes and oregano.

Serves 4.

■ Recipe best made just before serving.
■ Freeze: Not suitable.
■ Microwave: Suitable.

BAKED RICE AND RICOTTA GNOCCHI

2 cups cooked white short-grain rice
2 cups (400g) ricotta cheese
½ cup (40g) grated parmesan cheese
1 egg, lightly beaten
¼ cup (35g) plain flour
⅓ cup (50g) rice flour
1 teaspoon cracked black pepper
30g butter, melted
1 clove garlic, crushed
¼ cup (20g) grated parmesan cheese, extra
1 tablespoon pine nuts

Grease 19cm x 29cm rectangular slice pan, line base and sides with baking paper. Combine rice, ricotta and parmesan, egg, sifted flours and pepper; mix well. Spread mixture into prepared pan, cover, refrigerate several hours or overnight.

Turn rice mixture out of pan onto lightly floured surface, cut into 5cm rounds. Slightly overlap rounds in well-greased shallow ovenproof dish (1.5 litre/6 cup capacity). Brush well with combined butter and garlic, sprinkle with extra parmesan cheese and nuts. Bake, uncovered, in hot oven about 30 minutes or until browned.

Serves 4.

■ Recipe can be prepared a day ahead; bake just before serving.
■ Storage: Covered, in refrigerator.
■ Freeze: Cooked rice suitable.
■ Microwave: Rice suitable.

From back: Baked Rice and Ricotta Gnocchi, Mushroom and Sun-Dried Tomato Risotto.

Plates from House.

ROASTED EGGPLANT, PEPPER AND RICE SALAD

2 medium (600g) eggplants
coarse cooking salt
1 small (150g) red pepper, quartered
1 small (150g) yellow pepper,
    quartered
2 tablespoons olive oil
1 cup cooked brown rice and
    wild rice blend
½ cup (25g) firmly packed
    watercress sprigs
1 cup cooked white long-grain rice
2 small (100g) bocconcini
    cheese, sliced
12 cherry tomatoes, halved

DRESSING
1 egg yolk
1 tablespoon lemon juice
2 teaspoons balsamic vinegar
1½ teaspoons sugar
1 teaspoon chopped fresh tarragon
1 clove garlic, crushed
¾ cup (180ml) olive oil
2 tablespoons water, approximately

Cut eggplants into 1cm slices, place in colander, sprinkle with salt; stand 30 minutes. Rinse under cold water; drain on absorbent paper. Remove seeds and membranes from peppers.

Place eggplant slices and peppers, skin side up, on greased oven tray, brush with oil. Bake in moderately hot oven about 30 minutes or until eggplant slices and peppers are browned and tender; turn eggplant slices halfway during cooking; cool. Peel away skin from peppers, slice peppers.

Place some of the brown rice and wild rice blend on each serving plate, top with some of the peppers, watercress, white rice, eggplant slices and cheese, add tomatoes. Serve with dressing.

Dressing: Blend or process egg yolk, juice, vinegar, sugar, tarragon and garlic until smooth. Add oil gradually in a thin stream while motor is operating; blend until thick. Stir in enough water to give desired consistency.

Serves 4.

- Rice can be cooked a day ahead. Dressing can be made 3 days ahead.
- Storage: Covered, separately, in refrigerator.
- Freeze: Cooked rice suitable.
- Microwave: Rice suitable.

BELOW: Roasted Eggplant, Pepper and Rice Salad.

SPINACH RICE

30g butter
1 tablespoon olive oil
2 medium (300g) onions,
  finely chopped
2 cloves garlic, crushed
2 cups (400g) white long-grain rice
1 litre (4 cups) chicken stock
1 bunch (500g) English spinach,
  chopped
2 medium (260g) tomatoes, peeled,
  seeded, chopped
¼ cup (20g) grated parmesan cheese

Heat butter and oil in medium pan, add onions and garlic, cook, stirring, until onions are soft. Add rice, cook, stirring, 2 minutes. Add stock, simmer, covered, about 15 minutes or until liquid is almost absorbed. Remove from heat, stir in spinach, tomatoes and cheese, stir until spinach is wilted.

Serves 4 to 6.

■ Recipe best made just before serving.
■ Freeze: Not suitable.
■ Microwave: Suitable.

CURRY RICE

1 tablespoon vegetable oil
20g butter
1 medium (150g) onion, sliced
1½ cups (300g) basmati rice
2 cups (500ml) water
¾ cup (180ml) coconut milk
2 tablespoons chopped fresh
  coriander

CURRY PASTE
2 small fresh red chillies, chopped
1 tablespoon chopped fresh
  lemon grass
2 cloves garlic, crushed
2 teaspoons shrimp paste
1 teaspoon cumin seeds
½ teaspoon garam masala
½ teaspoon ground turmeric

Heat oil and butter in medium pan, add onion and curry paste, cook, stirring, until onion is soft. Stir in rice, then water and coconut milk, simmer, covered, about 15 minutes or until rice is tender, stirring occasionally. Stir in coriander.

Curry Paste: Blend or process all ingredients until well combined.

Serves 4 to 6.

■ Recipe best made close to serving.
■ Freeze: Not suitable.
■ Microwave: Suitable.

ABOVE: From left: Spinach Rice, Curry Rice.

Cloth, placemat, plates and tray from Sirocco Homewares; spoon from Orson & Blake.

83

BEST-EVER FRIED RICE

3 cups cooked white long-grain rice
1½ tablespoons peanut oil
3 eggs, lightly beaten
1 teaspoon sesame oil
2 medium (240g) carrots, sliced
1 medium (150g) onion, sliced
2 sticks celery, sliced
3 bacon rashers, chopped
1 clove garlic, crushed
1 tablespoon grated fresh ginger
150g Chinese barbecued pork, sliced
150g small cooked shelled prawns
425g can baby corn, drained, sliced
1 cup (125g) frozen peas
4 green shallots, chopped
1 tablespoon soy sauce

Heat remaining peanut oil and sesame oil in wok, add carrots, onion, celery, bacon, garlic and ginger, stir-fry over high heat until vegetables are just tender.

Spread rice over shallow tray; refrigerate, uncovered, overnight.

Add rice, omelette, and remaining ingredients to wok, stir-fry until well combined and heated through.

Serves 4 to 6.

- Rice best cooked a day ahead.
- Storage: Uncovered, in refrigerator.
- Freeze: Cooked rice suitable.
- Microwave: Rice suitable.

Heat 1 teaspoon of the peanut oil in wok or pan, add half the eggs, swirl wok so eggs form a thin omelette, cook until set. Transfer omelette to board, cut into strips. Repeat with 1 teaspoon of the remaining peanut oil and remaining eggs.

LEFT: Best-Ever Fried Rice.

Bowl, spoon and tea-towel from Orson & Blake.

RICE CAKE WITH CRISPY POTATOES AND DILL

40g butter
1 medium (150g) onion,
    finely chopped
1 bacon rasher, finely chopped
1 clove garlic, crushed
3 cups cooked basmati rice
130g can corn kernels, drained
2 tablespoons chopped fresh dill
¼ cup (20g) grated parmesan cheese
50g butter, extra
1 large (300g) old potato,
    peeled, sliced

Melt butter in 20cm non-stick frying pan. Add onion, bacon and garlic, cook, stirring, until onion is soft. Combine onion mixture, rice, corn, dill and cheese in bowl; mix well. Melt half the extra butter in same pan, remove from heat. Slightly overlap potato slices over base of pan. Place pan over medium heat and spoon rice mixture over potatoes, pressing down lightly. Dot with remaining butter. Cook, covered, 5 minutes on medium heat. Reduce heat to low, cook, covered, 45 minutes. Stand 10 minutes before turning onto a serving plate.

Serves 4 to 6.

■ Recipe best made close to serving.
■ Freeze: Not suitable.
■ Microwave: Rice suitable.

ABOVE: From left: Rice Cake with Crispy Potatoes and Dill, Peanut and Sunflower Seed Pilaf.
RIGHT: Rosemary and Parmesan Rice Chips.

Right: Setting from Barbara's Storehouse.

PEANUT AND SUNFLOWER SEED PILAF

1 litre (4 cups) chicken stock
4 cardamom pods
1 teaspoon cumin seeds
1 cinnamon stick
¼ teaspoon dried crushed chillies
pinch saffron powder
2 cups (400g) basmati rice
¼ cup (35g) roasted unsalted peanuts
1 tablespoon sunflower seed kernels, toasted

Combine stock, cardamom, cumin, cinnamon, chillies and saffron in medium pan, bring to boil, add rice, reduce heat to low, cover, simmer about 12 minutes or until liquid is absorbed. Discard cardamom and cinnamon. Serve pilaf sprinkled with peanuts and seeds.

Serves 4.

■ Recipe best made just before serving.
■ Freeze: Not suitable.
■ Microwave: Suitable.

ROSEMARY AND PARMESAN RICE CHIPS

1 tablespoon olive oil
1 small (80g) onion, finely chopped
1 tablespoon chopped fresh rosemary
1½ cups (300g) white short-grain rice
3 cups (750ml) chicken stock
½ cup (40g) grated parmesan cheese
cornflour
vegetable oil for deep-frying

Grease 20cm x 30cm lamington pan, place strip of baking paper to cover base and extend over 2 opposite sides.

Heat olive oil in medium pan, add onion and rosemary, cook, stirring, until onion is soft. Add rice, cook, stirring, until all the grains are coated in onion mixture. Add stock, simmer, covered, about 15 minutes or until rice is just tender. Remove from heat, stand, covered, 5 minutes. Stir in cheese. Press mixture evenly and firmly into prepared pan, cover, refrigerate about 3 hours or until firm

Remove rice mixture from pan, cut lengthways into 3 pieces, then carefully cut each third into 1.5cm wide chips. Dust chips with cornflour, shake away excess cornflour. Deep-fry chips gently in batches in hot vegetable oil until golden brown and crisp; drain on absorbent paper. Serve sprinkled with a little salt, if desired.

Makes about 60.

■ Recipe can be prepared a day ahead. Fry chips just before serving.
■ Storage: Covered, in refrigerator.
■ Freeze: Not suitable.
■ Microwave: Rice suitable.

KUMARA AND FENNEL RISOTTO

2 tablespoons olive oil
1 medium (150g) onion, chopped
1 clove garlic, crushed
1⅓ cups (265g) arborio rice
pinch saffron powder
¼ medium (150g) fennel bulb, sliced
1.5 litres (6 cups) chicken stock
150g kumara, sliced
⅓ cup (25g) grated parmesan cheese
¼ cup chopped fresh chives

Heat oil in large pan, add onion and garlic, cook, stirring, until onion is soft. Stir in rice, saffron and fennel. Bring stock to boil in separate pan; keep hot. Stir ⅔ cup (160ml) hot stock into rice mixture, cook, stirring, over low heat until liquid is absorbed. Continue adding stock gradually, stirring until absorbed before next addition. When about half the stock has been added, add kumara, cook, stirring, while adding remaining stock in stages. Total cooking time should be about 35 minutes or until rice is tender. Serve sprinkled with cheese and chives.

Serves 4 to 6.

■ Recipe best made close to serving.
■ Freeze: Not suitable.
■ Microwave: Suitable.

ROASTED PEPPER AND GARLIC RICE

2 medium (400g) red peppers
2 tablespoons olive oil
2 cloves garlic, crushed
½ cup (125ml) dry white wine
2 cups (400g) white short-grain rice
3½ cups (875ml) chicken stock
⅓ cup (80ml) cream
½ cup (80g) seedless black olives
2 teaspoons chopped fresh sage

Quarter peppers, remove seeds and membranes. Grill peppers, skin side up, until skin blisters and blackens. Peel away skin; chop peppers. Blend or process peppers, oil, garlic and wine until combined. Add pepper mixture to large pan, stir over heat until mixture boils. Add rice,

CURRIED CHICKPEAS AND RICE

1 cup (200g) dried chickpeas
1 tablespoon peanut oil
2 medium (300g) onions,
　finely chopped
2 cloves garlic, crushed
2 tablespoons medium hot
　curry paste
2 cups (500ml) chicken stock
1 tablespoon mango chutney
1 cup (250ml) coconut cream
2 cups cooked brown rice
1/4 cup chopped fresh coriander

Place chickpeas in large bowl, cover well with water, cover, stand overnight.

Drain chickpeas, rinse well. Place chickpeas in pan, cover with water, simmer, uncovered, 40 minutes; drain.

Heat oil in medium pan, add onions, garlic and paste, cook, stirring, until onions are soft. Add chickpeas and stock, simmer, uncovered, 10 minutes or until chickpeas are tender. Add chutney and coconut cream, simmer 10 minutes. Stir in rice and coriander.

Serves 4 to 6.

■ Recipe can be prepared a day ahead.
■ Storage: Covered, in refrigerator.
■ Freeze: Not suitable.
■ Microwave: Rice suitable.

INDIAN RICE PANCAKE

6 cups hot cooked basmati rice
2 cloves garlic, crushed
2 teaspoons grated fresh ginger
1 1/2 teaspoons garam masala
2 teaspoons ground cumin
3 eggs, lightly beaten
1/3 cup (50g) brown rice flour
40g ghee

Combine rice, garlic, ginger, spices, eggs and flour in bowl; mix well. Heat ghee in non-stick 25cm frying pan, add rice mixture; press evenly over base of pan. Cook over low heat until browned underneath and firm. Invert onto serving plate. Cut into wedges to serve.

Serves 6.

■ Recipe best made just before serving.
■ Freeze: Cooked rice suitable.
■ Microwave: Rice suitable.

stir until rice is coated with pepper mixture. Stir in stock, simmer, covered, about 15 minutes or until rice is tender. Stir in cream, olives and sage, stir over heat until mixture is thick and creamy.

Serves 6.

■ Recipe best made just before serving.
■ Freeze: Not suitable.
■ Microwave: Rice mixture suitable.

ABOVE: From left: Roasted Pepper and Garlic Rice, Kumara and Fennel Risotto.
RIGHT: From back: Curried Chickpeas and Rice, Indian Rice Pancake.

Right: Wire basket, terracotta bowls, wooden servers and cushion cover from Morris Home & Garden Wares; tiles from Country Floors.

JASMINE RICE SALAD WITH CHILLI COCONUT DRESSING

¼ cup (50g) uncooked jasmine rice
1 small (130g) green cucumber
3 small (270g) zucchini
1 small (150g) red pepper
1 medium (430g) mango
2 green shallots
1½ cups cooked jasmine rice
¼ cup loosely packed fresh
    coriander leaves

CHILLI COCONUT DRESSING
2 small fresh red chillies
1 clove garlic, crushed
⅓ cup (80ml) coconut milk
¼ cup loosely packed fresh
    mint leaves
1 tablespoon honey
2 teaspoons fish sauce

Place uncooked rice in pan, cook, stirring, until lightly browned; cool. Blend or process rice until coarsely ground. Cut cucumber in half lengthways, remove seeds. Cut cucumber, zucchini, pepper, mango and shallots into 6cm lengths, cut into strips.

Combine cucumber, zucchini, pepper, mango, shallots, cooked rice and coriander in bowl; mix well. Just before serving, drizzle with dressing, top with ground rice.
Chilli Coconut Dressing: Blend or process all ingredients until combined.

Serves 4 to 6.

- ■ Salad and dressing can be made a day ahead.
- ■ Storage: Covered, separately, in refrigerator.
- ■ Freeze: Cooked rice suitable.
- ■ Microwave: Rice suitable.

BARBECUED PORK SALAD

100g snow peas, halved
3 cups cooked brown rice
425g can baby corn, drained
230g can water chestnuts, drained
1 small (150g) red pepper, chopped
4 green shallots, chopped
150g Chinese barbecued pork, sliced
1 tablespoon sesame seeds, toasted

DRESSING
¼ cup (60ml) peanut oil
2 teaspoons sesame oil
1 teaspoon salt-reduced soy sauce
¼ cup (60ml) rice vinegar
1 clove garlic, crushed
½ teaspoon brown sugar

Boil, steam or microwave snow peas until just tender; drain. Combine snow peas, rice, chopped corn, halved chestnuts, pepper, shallots and pork in bowl. Add dressing; top with sesame seeds.
Dressing: Combine all ingredients in jar; shake well.

Serves 4.

- Salad can be made a day ahead.
- Storage: Covered, in refrigerator.
- Freeze: Cooked rice suitable.
- Microwave: Rice suitable.

SMOKED CHEESE AND RICE PEARS

25g mozzarella cheese
20g butter
1 medium (150g) onion, finely chopped
2 teaspoons chopped fresh thyme
2 teaspoons Cajun seasoning
4½ cups cooked white short-grain rice
¾ cup (90g) grated smoked cheddar cheese
1 egg
plain flour
2 eggs, lightly beaten, extra
½ cup (50g) packaged breadcrumbs, approximately
vegetable oil for deep-frying
10 cloves
10 small fresh oregano leaves

Cut mozzarella cheese into 10 small cubes. Heat butter in small pan, add onion, thyme and seasoning, cook, stirring, until onion is soft. Process rice, onion mixture, smoked cheese and egg until mixture is roughly chopped.

Divide mixture into 10 portions, press a mozzarella cube into centre of each portion. Using floured hands, shape mixture into pear shapes, coat in flour, shake away excess flour. Dip pears into extra eggs, then into breadcrumbs, shake away excess crumbs. Deep-fry pears slowly in batches in hot oil, so they have time to heat through to the centre; drain on absorbent paper. Press a clove and an oregano leaf into the top of each pear.

Makes 10.

- Recipe best prepared a day ahead. Cook just before serving.
- Storage: Covered, in refrigerator.
- Freeze: Rice suitable.
- Microwave: Rice suitable.

LEFT: From back: Barbecued Pork Salad, Jasmine Rice Salad with Chilli Coconut Dressing.
ABOVE: Smoked Cheese and Rice Pears.

Left: Setting from Barbara's Storehouse.

TOMATO HERB RICE

2 teaspoons olive oil
1 medium (150g) onion, chopped
2 cloves garlic, crushed
1½ cups (300g) white long-grain rice
2¾ cups (680ml) water
½ cup (125ml) tomato paste
1 tablespoon chopped fresh basil

Heat oil in medium heavy-based pan, add onion and garlic, cook, stirring, until onion is soft. Stir in rice, then water, simmer, covered, 12 minutes. Stir in paste and basil. Remove from heat, stand, covered, 10 minutes.

Serves 4.

■ Recipe best made just before serving.
■ Freeze: Suitable.
■ Microwave: Suitable.

INDIAN RICE

2 teaspoons peanut oil
1 medium (150g) onion, chopped
1 clove garlic, crushed
½ teaspoon ground turmeric
1 teaspoon ground coriander
1 teaspoon ground cumin
1 teaspoon garam masala
1½ cups (300g) white long-grain rice
3 cups (750ml) chicken stock

Heat oil in medium heavy-based pan, add onion and garlic, cook, stirring, until onion is soft. Add spices, cook, stirring, until fragrant. Stir in rice, then stock, simmer, covered, 12 minutes. Remove from heat, stand, covered, 10 minutes.

Serves 4.

■ Recipe best made just before serving.
■ Freeze: Suitable.
■ Microwave: Suitable

ABOVE: Clockwise from top: Tomato Herb Rice, Indian Rice, Middle Eastern Rice.

MIDDLE EASTERN RICE

2 teaspoons vegetable oil
1 medium (150g) onion, chopped
1 teaspoon allspice
1 teaspoon ground cumin
½ teaspoon ground cinnamon
¼ teaspoon chilli powder
1½ cups (300g) white long-grain rice
3 cups (750ml) chicken stock

Heat oil in medium heavy-based pan, add onion, cook, stirring, until onion is soft. Add spices, cook, stirring, until fragrant. Stir in rice, then stock, simmer, covered, 12 minutes. Remove from heat, stand, covered, 10 minutes.

Serves 4.

■ Recipe best made just before serving.
■ Freeze: Suitable.
■ Microwave: Suitable.

BELOW: From left: Spicy Satay Rice, Herbed Rice.

SPICY SATAY RICE

2 tablespoons peanut oil
2 medium (300g) onions, sliced
2 cloves garlic, crushed
1 teaspoon grated fresh ginger
½ teaspoon sambal oelek
1 teaspoon ground cumin
1 teaspoon ground coriander
2 teaspoons mild curry powder
2 cups (400g) jasmine rice
¼ cup (65g) smooth peanut butter
¾ cup (180ml) coconut milk
3⅓ cups (830ml) chicken stock
½ cup (75g) unsalted roasted peanuts
2 tablespoons chopped fresh coriander

Heat oil in medium pan, add onions, garlic, ginger, sambal oelek and spices, cook, stirring, until onions are soft. Stir in rice, then peanut butter, coconut milk, and stock, simmer, covered, 10 minutes. Remove from heat, stand, covered, 10 minutes. Stir in remaining ingredients.

Serves 6.

■ Recipe best made just before serving.
■ Freeze: Not suitable.
■ Microwave: Suitable.

HERBED RICE

2 tablespoons olive oil
2 cloves garlic, crushed
1 tablespoon chopped fresh rosemary
1 medium (200g) red Spanish onion, finely chopped
¼ cup firmly packed fresh parsley sprigs
⅓ cup chopped fresh chives
1½ tablespoons balsamic vinegar
½ teaspoon sugar
6 cups cooked white short-grain rice

Heat half the oil in pan, add garlic, rosemary and onion, cook, stirring, until onion is soft. Combine onion mixture with parsley, chives, remaining oil, vinegar, sugar and rice in bowl. Serve hot or cold.

Serves 4 to 6.

■ Recipe can be made a day ahead.
■ Storage: Covered, in refrigerator.
■ Freeze: Suitable.
■ Microwave: Rice suitable.

TRIPLE RICE SALAD

1 cup cooked wild rice
1 cup cooked brown rice
3 cups cooked jasmine rice
1 medium (200g) yellow pepper,
   finely chopped
4 green shallots, chopped
2 large (500g) tomatoes, peeled,
   seeded, chopped

DRESSING
1 clove garlic, crushed
2 tablespoons chopped fresh mint
2 tablespoons chopped fresh
   coriander
½ teaspoon sugar
½ cup (125ml) olive oil
¼ cup (60ml) lemon juice

Combine all the rice, pepper, shallots and
tomatoes in bowl, add dressing; mix well.
Cover, refrigerate 1 hour before serving.
Dressing: Combine all ingredients in jar;
shake well.

Serves 4 to 6.

■ Recipe can be made a day ahead.
■ Storage: Covered, in refrigerator.
■ Freeze: Cooked rice suitable.
■ Microwave: Rice suitable.

RICE AND AVOCADO SALAD

1 medium (200g) red pepper
6 cups cooked white long-grain rice
1 small (100g) red Spanish onion,
   chopped
3 thin slices (45g) hot pancetta,
   finely chopped
2 tablespoons pine nuts, toasted
¼ cup chopped fresh basil
1 medium (250g) avocado, chopped

DRESSING
2 tablespoons red wine vinegar
⅓ cup (80ml) olive oil
1 clove garlic, crushed
¼ teaspoon sugar

Quarter pepper, remove seeds and
membranes. Grill pepper, skin side up,
until skin blisters and blackens. Peel away
skin, chop pepper finely. Combine all ingredients with dressing in bowl; mix well.
Dressing: Place all ingredients in jar;
shake well.

Serves 6.

■ Recipe, without avocado, can be
   prepared a day ahead; add
   avocado just before serving.
■ Storage: Covered, in refrigerator.
■ Freeze: Cooked rice suitable.
■ Microwave: Rice suitable.

SWEET MOROCCAN RICE

1 cup (150g) broad beans
1 cup (200g) basmati rice
2 teaspoons orange flower water
1½ cups (375ml) water
2 tablespoons vegetable oil
1 medium (150g) onion, chopped
1 teaspoon ground turmeric
1 teaspoon grated fresh ginger
425g can tomatoes
390g can artichoke hearts,
   drained, quartered
1 medium (200g) green pepper, sliced
1 teaspoon grated orange rind
1 tablespoon chopped fresh parsley

Boil, steam or microwave beans until
tender; drain, peel. Combine rice,
orange flower water and water in medium pan, bring to boil, simmer, covered,
12 minutes. Remove from heat, stand,
covered, 10 minutes. Heat oil in pan, add
onion, turmeric and ginger, cook, stirring, until onion is soft. Add undrained
crushed tomatoes, beans and remaining ingredients, stir until hot.

Serves 4.

■ Recipe can be made 3 hours ahead.
■ Storage: Covered, in refrigerator.
■ Freeze: Not suitable.
■ Microwave: Suitable.

MEXICAN-STYLE RICE

1 medium (130g) tomato, peeled,
    seeded, chopped
1 tablespoon vegetable oil
1 clove garlic, chopped
1 small (80g) onion, chopped
1½ cups (300g) white long-grain rice
1 tablespoon tomato paste
3 cups (750ml) hot chicken stock
1 small (70g) carrot, finely sliced
2 teaspoons drained chopped
    jalapeno peppers
½ cup (60g) frozen peas
2 tablespoons chopped fresh
    coriander

Blend or process tomato until smooth. Heat oil in medium pan, add garlic, onion and rice, cook, stirring, until onion is soft and rice lightly browned. Stir in tomato puree, paste, stock, carrot and peppers, simmer, covered, 12 minutes. Add peas, cook, covered, few minutes or until rice is tender. Remove from heat, stand, covered, 10 minutes. Stir in coriander.

Serves 4 to 6.

■ Recipe best made just before serving.
■ Freeze: Not suitable.
■ Microwave: Suitable.

LEFT: From left: Triple Rice Salad, Rice and Avocado Salad.
BELOW: From left: Sweet Moroccan Rice, Mexican-Style Rice.

Below: Plates from House.

WILD RICE WITH BROAD BEANS AND RED PEPPER

1½ cups (300g) white long-grain rice
⅓ cup (60g) wild rice
1 large (350g) red pepper
2 tablespoons olive oil
20g butter
1 small (200g) leek, chopped
1 teaspoon ground cumin
**3 cups (450g) frozen broad beans,
   thawed, peeled**
1 tablespoon chopped fresh parsley
2½ cups (625ml) chicken stock

Soak all the rice together in large bowl of cold water 2 hours.

Drain rice. Quarter pepper, remove seeds and membranes. Grill pepper, skin side up, until skin blisters and blackens. Peel away skin, slice pepper.

Heat oil and butter in large pan, add leek, cumin, beans, parsley and pepper, cook, stirring, until leek is soft. Stir in rice, then stock, simmer, covered, about 25 minutes or until rice is tender. Remove from heat, stand, covered, 5 minutes.

Serves 4 to 6.

■ Recipe best made close to serving.
■ Freeze: Not suitable.
■ Microwave: Suitable.

ASPARAGUS MUSHROOM SALAD WITH RICE PESTO

500g asparagus spears, halved
¼ cup (60ml) olive oil
500g button mushrooms
2 tablespoons drained capers
1 tablespoon balsamic vinegar
2 tablespoons lemon juice
2 cloves garlic, crushed
1½ cups cooked brown rice
¼ cup (20g) flaked parmesan cheese

RICE PESTO

**1½ cups firmly packed fresh
   basil leaves**
¼ cup (20g) grated parmesan cheese
2 tablespoons pine nuts, toasted
1 tablespoon lemon juice
⅓ cup (80ml) olive oil

Add asparagus to pan of boiling water; drain immediately, rinse under cold water; drain. Heat oil in pan, add mushrooms, cook, stirring, until lightly browned. Combine asparagus, mushrooms, capers, vinegar, juice and garlic in bowl; mix well. Cover, refrigerate 1 hour.

Drain mushroom mixture, reserve ¼ cup (60ml) of marinade for pesto. Reserve ⅓ cup of rice for pesto. Combine mushroom mixture and remaining rice. Top with rice pesto and cheese.

Rice Pesto: Blend or process reserved ⅓ cup rice, reserved marinade, basil, cheese, nuts and juice until combined. Add oil gradually in a thin stream while motor is operating.

Serves 4 to 6.

■ Salad and pesto can be made
   3 hours ahead.
■ Storage: Covered, separately,
   in refrigerator.
■ Freeze: Not suitable.
■ Microwave: Asparagus and
   rice suitable.

LEFT: From left: Wild Rice with Broad Beans and Red Pepper, Asparagus Mushroom Salad with Rice Pesto.

NASI GORENG

10g butter
2 eggs, lightly beaten
1 tablespoon peanut oil
1 clove garlic, crushed
1 small fresh red chilli, finely chopped
4 green shallots, chopped
150g chicken thigh fillets, chopped
150g button mushrooms, sliced
150g Chinese barbecued pork, sliced
1 small (70g) carrot, thinly sliced
200g cooked shelled prawns
4 cups cooked jasmine rice
6 English spinach leaves, shredded
1 tablespoon soy sauce
1 tablespoon tomato sauce
1 teaspoon hot paprika

Heat butter in wok or pan, add eggs, swirl wok so eggs form a thin omelette, cook until just set, remove from wok; cool. Roll omelette, cut into 5mm slices. Heat oil in wok, add garlic, chilli and shallots, cook, stirring, until shallots are just tender. Add chicken, cook, stirring, until chicken is tender. Add mushrooms, pork, carrot, prawns, rice and spinach, cook, stirring, until combined and hot. Stir in sauces and paprika. Serve topped with omelette.

Serves 4 to 6.

- Recipe can be made a day ahead.
- Storage: Covered, in refrigerator.
- Freeze: Not suitable.
- Microwave: Rice suitable.

HERB AND BACON RICE

¼ cup (60ml) olive oil
2 bacon rashers, chopped
2 medium (240g) zucchini, grated
6 green shallots, chopped
6 cups cooked white long-grain rice
¼ cup chopped fresh chives
¼ cup chopped fresh parsley

Heat oil in large pan, add bacon, cook, stirring, until bacon is crisp. Add zucchini and shallots, cook, stirring, until zucchini is tender. Add rice and herbs; mix well.

Serves 6.

- Recipe can be prepared a day ahead.
- Storage: Covered, in refrigerator.
- Freeze: Not suitable.
- Microwave: Suitable.

COCONUT RICE

40g ghee
1 clove garlic, crushed
1 teaspoon cumin seeds
1 medium (150g) onion, sliced
2 cups (400g) basmati rice
1½ cups (375ml) coconut milk
1⅓ cups (330ml) chicken stock

Heat ghee in large, heavy-based pan, add garlic, seeds and onion, cook, stirring, until onion is soft. Add rice, cook, stirring, 2 minutes. Stir in coconut milk and stock, simmer, covered, about 12 minutes or until rice is just tender. Remove from heat, stand, covered, 10 minutes.

Serves 6.

- Recipe best made just before serving.
- Freeze: Suitable.
- Microwave: Suitable.

SAFFRON RICE

1⅓ cups (265g) basmati rice
1.25 litres (5 cups) water
¼ teaspoon saffron threads
50g butter
½ teaspoon ground cumin
½ teaspoon ground cardamom
½ teaspoon ground coriander

Combine rice, water and saffron in pan, boil, uncovered, until rice is just tender; drain. Spread rice on tray covered with baking paper; cool. Heat butter in large pan, add spices, cook, stirring, until fragrant. Stir in rice.

Serves 4 to 6.

- Recipe can be made a day ahead.
- Storage: Covered, in refrigerator.
- Freeze: Suitable.
- Microwave: Suitable.

ABOVE: Nasi Goreng.
RIGHT: Clockwise from back: Herb and Bacon Rice, Coconut Rice, Saffron Rice.

Above: Setting from Sirocco Homewares.
Right: Placemats, bottles and bowls from Hale Imports.

·Desserts·

Let us tempt you with luscious hazelnut and caramel rice ice-cream, scrumptious cakes, souffles, and a lemon meringue rice pie – plus our versions of all the favourite rice puddings. For helpful rice cooking tips, turn to page 120.

DOUBLE NUT CAKE WITH COFFEE CREME ANGLAISE

200g butter
1 cup (220g) caster sugar
4 eggs
¾ cup (105g) self-raising flour
½ cup (75g) rice flour
½ cup (60g) packaged ground almonds
¼ cup (30g) chopped toasted hazelnuts
¼ cup (60ml) brandy or Frangelico

COFFEE CREME ANGLAISE
1¾ cups (430ml) milk
300ml thickened cream
¾ cup (65g) roasted coffee beans
4 egg yolks
⅓ cup (65g) firmly packed brown sugar

Grease deep 20cm round cake pan, cover base with baking paper. Cream butter and sugar in medium bowl with electric mixer, beat in eggs 1 at a time. Stir in sifted flours, nuts and brandy in 2 batches.

Spread mixture into prepared pan, bake in moderate oven about 50 minutes or until firm. Turn cake onto wire rack to cool. Top cake with whipped cream and toasted flaked almonds, if desired. Serve with coffee creme anglaise.

Coffee Creme Anglaise: Combine milk, cream and beans in medium pan, bring to boil, remove from heat, cover, stand 1 hour. Strain mixture, discard beans. Whisk egg yolks and sugar in small bowl until thick and pale, whisk in milk mixture. Return mixture to pan, stir over heat, without boiling, until slightly thickened; cool.

- Recipe can be made a day ahead.
- Storage: Cake, in airtight container. Creme anglaise, covered, in refrigerator.
- Freeze: Cake suitable.
- Microwave: Not suitable.

CHOCOLATE PISTACHIO RICE CAKE

This cake does not contain flour.

1½ cups cooked brown rice
4 eggs, separated
1 cup (220g) caster sugar
1 teaspoon grated lemon rind
200g dark chocolate, melted
90g unsalted butter, melted
2 cups (250g) packaged ground almonds
½ cup (60g) shelled chopped pistachios
¼ cup (60ml) orange juice
2 tablespoons chopped glace ginger

Grease 22cm springform tin, line base and side with baking paper.

Combine rice and 1 of the egg yolks in bowl, press mixture over base of prepared tin. Beat remaining yolks, sugar and rind in small bowl with electric mixer until thick and creamy. Fold in cooled chocolate and butter, nuts, juice and ginger. Beat egg whites in small bowl with electric mixer until soft peaks form, fold into chocolate mixture in 2 batches. Pour mixture over rice base in tin, bake in moderate oven about 1½ hours or until firm; cool in tin. Serve dusted with sifted icing sugar, if desired.

- Recipe best made a day ahead.
- Storage: Covered, in refrigerator.
- Freeze: Suitable.
- Microwave: Chocolate and butter suitable.

From back: Chocolate Pistachio Rice Cake, Double Nut Cake with Coffee Creme Anglaise.

Tiles from Country Floors.

RICE ANISE TERRINE WITH SUMMER FRUITS

150g raspberries
1/3 cup (75g) sugar
2 teaspoons lemon juice
1 cup (250ml) water
1 tablespoon gelatine
425ml can coconut milk
1/2 cup (110g) sugar, extra
1 tablespoon finely chopped fresh
    lemon grass
2 star anise
1 cup (200g) white short-grain rice
250g strawberries, chopped
200g blueberries

Oil 14cm x 21cm loaf pan. Combine raspberries, sugar, juice and 1/4 cup (60ml) of the water in small pan, stir over heat, without boiling, until sugar is dissolved. Bring to boil, simmer, uncovered, about 5 minutes or until pulpy. Sprinkle gelatine over another 1/4 cup (60ml) of the water in small cup, stand in pan of simmering water, stir until dissolved. Push raspberry mixture through fine sieve, stir in gelatine mixture.

Combine coconut milk, remaining water, extra sugar, lemon grass and anise in medium pan, stir over heat, without boiling, until sugar is dissolved. Bring to boil, add rice, cover, simmer

about 20 minutes or until nearly all the liquid is absorbed; stand, covered, 10 minutes. Discard anise. Process mixture until roughly chopped.

Press half the rice mixture over base of prepared pan with a wet spatula, top with strawberries and blueberries, pour raspberry mixture over rice layer. Carefully spread remaining rice mixture over berry mixture. Cover, refrigerate several hours or overnight until set.

Serves 4 to 6.

■ Recipe best made a day ahead.
■ Storage: Covered, in refrigerator.
■ Freeze: Not suitable.
■ Microwave: Suitable.

102

WALNUT AND RICE SHORTBREAD BUTTERFLIES

90g butter, chopped
2 tablespoons caster sugar
1 tablespoon maple-flavoured syrup
¼ cup (35g) rice flour
⅔ cup (100g) plain flour
¼ cup (30g) finely chopped
    toasted walnuts
icing sugar mixture

MANGO MOUSSE
1 medium (430g) mango, chopped
1 cup (250g) mascarpone cheese
½ cup (80g) icing sugar mixture
2 tablespoons lime juice
2 teaspoons gelatine
1 tablespoon water
few drops yellow or orange food
    colouring

Beat butter, sugar and maple syrup in medium bowl with electric mixer until smooth. Stir in sifted flours and nuts in 2 batches. Knead dough gently on lightly floured surface until smooth, cover, refrigerate 30 minutes. Roll dough between sheets of baking paper until 4mm thick. Cut dough into 6cm crescent shapes, place about 3cm apart on greased oven trays. Bake in moderate oven about 10 minutes or until lightly browned. Stand few minutes before lifting onto wire racks to cool. You will need 16 crescents for this recipe; reserve remaining crescents for another use.

Lightly dust crescents with icing sugar. Place 4 crescents on each serving plate to resemble butterfly wings, pipe mango mousse to resemble bodies. Slice reserved mango (from mousse) into thin strips for feelers. Serve with extra fresh fruit, if desired.

Mango Mousse: Reserve a small piece of mango. Blend or process remaining mango until smooth. Combine cheese, sifted sugar and juice in bowl, gently fold in mango. Sprinkle gelatine over water in cup, stand in small pan of simmering water, stir until dissolved. Combine gelatine mixture, mango mixture and a few drops of food colouring if desired; mix well. Refrigerate mango mixture about 1 hour or until firm enough to pipe. Spoon mango mixture into piping bag fitted with medium plain tube.

Serves 4.

- ■ Shortbread can be made 3 days ahead. Mousse best made close to serving.
- ■ Storage: Shortbread, in airtight container.
- ■ Freeze: Uncooked shortbread dough suitable.
- ■ Microwave: Gelatine suitable.

LEFT: Rice Anise Terrine with Summer Fruits.
BELOW: Walnut and Rice Shortbread Butterflies.

Left: Setting from House. Below: Plates from Country Road Homewear.

COFFEE RICE BRULEE

600ml thickened cream
⅔ cup (60g) roasted coffee beans
1 cup cooked white short-grain rice
5 egg yolks
¼ cup (50g) brown sugar
1 tablespoon maple-flavoured syrup
⅓ cup (65g) firmly packed brown
  sugar, extra

Combine cream with coffee beans in pan, bring to boil, remove from heat, cover, stand 1 hour.

Divide rice between 4 ovenproof dishes (1 cup/250ml capacity). Beat egg yolks, sugar and maple syrup in small bowl with electric mixer until pale and thick. Gradually pour in coffee mixture. Return mixture to pan, stir over heat, without boiling, until slightly thickened; strain, discard coffee beans. Pour coffee mixture into prepared dishes; refrigerate until set.

Sprinkle extra brown sugar over set custard about 1 hour before serving. Place dishes in lamington pan. Place ice cubes around dishes, grill until sugar is lightly browned and melted. Refrigerate until ready to serve. Sprinkle with toasted flaked almonds, if desired.

Serves 4.

- Coffee mixture can be prepared a day ahead.
- Storage: Covered, in refrigerator.
- Freeze: Not suitable.
- Microwave: Not suitable.

MOIST BANANA RICE CAKE

You will need about 2 large (460g)
over-ripe bananas.

1½ cups (225g) plain flour
¾ cup (165g) caster sugar
½ teaspoon ground ginger
½ teaspoon ground cinnamon
½ teaspoon bicarbonate of soda
3 eggs, lightly beaten
¾ cup (180ml) vegetable oil
¾ cup (90g) chopped walnuts
1 cup mashed bananas
½ cup cooked white short-grain rice

TOPPING
30g butter, melted
1 cup (70g) shredded coconut
2 tablespoons honey, warmed

Grease deep 22cm round cake pan, cover base with baking paper, grease paper. Sift flour, sugar, spices and soda into large bowl, stir in remaining ingredients. Pour mixture into prepared pan, bake in moderate oven 50 minutes. Spread evenly with topping, bake 10 minutes or until topping is browned. Stand cake 10 minutes before turning onto wire rack to cool.
Topping: Combine all ingredients in bowl; mix well.

- Cake can be made 3 days ahead.
- Storage: Airtight container.
- Freeze: Suitable.
- Microwave: Not suitable.

CONTINENTAL RICE CAKE

4 eggs, separated
⅓ cup (75g) caster sugar
1 teaspoon grated orange rind
½ cup (75g) rice flour
⅓ cup (40g) packaged ground
  almonds
¼ cup (60ml) orange juice
2 tablespoons Cointreau

FILLING
300ml thickened cream
½ teaspoon grated orange rind
2 teaspoons caster sugar

Grease deep 20cm round cake pan, line base with baking paper, grease paper. Beat egg yolks, sugar and rind in small bowl with electric mixer until pale and thick, transfer mixture to large bowl. Fold in flour, nuts and juice.

Beat egg whites in small bowl with electric mixer until soft peaks form, fold into cake mixture in 2 batches. Pour mixture into prepared pan, bake in moderate oven about 25 minutes. Stand 5 minutes

before turning onto wire rack to cool. Split cake in half, brush half with liqueur. Spoon filling into piping bag fitted with star tube. Pipe filling onto half the cake, top with remaining cake, dust with sifted icing sugar, if desired. Decorate cake with extra whipped cream, shredded orange rind and crystallised violets, if desired.
Filling: Beat cream, rind and sugar in small bowl with electric mixer until firm peaks form.

- Recipe best made on day of serving.
- Storage: Covered, in refrigerator.
- Freeze: Unfilled cake suitable.
- Microwave: Not suitable.

LEFT: From back: Continental Rice Cake, Moist Banana Rice Cake.
ABOVE: Coffee Rice Brulee.

Left: Plates from Country Road Homewear.

DATE AND BUTTERSCOTCH SOUFFLES

**2 tablespoons finely chopped
    seedless dates**
1 tablespoon brandy
50g butter
1 tablespoon plain flour
¾ cup (180ml) milk
¼ cup (50g) brown sugar
1 cup cooked white short-grain rice
3 eggs, separated
1 tablespoon caster sugar

Combine dates and brandy in small bowl, stand 1 hour. Grease 4 souffle dishes (1 cup/250ml capacity), place on oven tray.

Melt butter in small pan, stir in flour, cook, stirring, 1 minute. Remove from heat, gradually stir in milk, stir over heat until mixture boils and thickens. Remove from heat, stir in brown sugar, rice, egg yolks and date mixture. Transfer mixture to large bowl.

Beat egg whites in small bowl with electric mixer until soft peaks form, add caster sugar, beat until dissolved. Fold egg whites into rice mixture, pour mixture into prepared dishes. Bake in moderately hot oven about 20 minutes or until browned; serve immediately.

Serves 4.

- Recipe must be made just before serving.
- Freeze: Not suitable.
- Microwave: Rice suitable.

MOCHA RISOTTO

½ cup (125ml) strong black coffee
3 cups (750ml) milk
⅔ cup (130g) arborio rice
½ cup (110g) caster sugar
80g dark chocolate, grated
2 teaspoons grated lemon rind

Combine coffee, milk, rice and sugar in medium heavy-based pan. Simmer gently, uncovered, stirring often, about 40 minutes or until mixture is thickened and rice tender. Stir in chocolate and rind. Serve warm with cream.

Serves 4.

- Recipe best made just before serving.
- Freeze: Not suitable.
- Microwave: Suitable.

MEXICAN-STYLE RICE PUDDING

1 medium lime
1 cinnamon stick
1 vanilla bean, split
2 cups (500ml) water
1 cup (200g) white long-grain rice
1 litre (4 cups) milk
⅔ cup (150g) sugar
2 egg yolks
¼ cup (40g) raisins
20g butter

Peel 4 strips of rind from lime. Combine rind, cinnamon, vanilla and water in medium heavy-based pan. Bring to boil, add rice, simmer, covered, about 15 minutes or until liquid is absorbed and rice tender.

Stir in milk and sugar, simmer, uncovered, stirring often, about 25 minutes or until mixture thickens. Remove from heat, discard rind, cinnamon and vanilla. Stir in yolks and half the raisins. Spoon mixture into ovenproof dish (1.25 litre/5 cup capacity), dot with butter, grill until lightly browned. Serve with remaining raisins and berries, if desired.

Serves 4 to 6.

- Recipe can be made 3 hours ahead.
- Storage: Covered, in refrigerator.
- Freeze: Not suitable.
- Microwave: Suitable.

LEFT: Date and Butterscotch Souffle.
RIGHT: From back: Mocha Risotto, Mexican-Style Rice Pudding.

Left: Dish from The Bay Tree Kitchen Shop.
Right: Setting from House.

LEMON MERINGUE RICE PIE

125g plain sweet biscuits
3 (30g) rice cakes
½ cup (45g) coconut
150g butter, melted

FILLING
400g can sweetened condensed milk
½ cup (125ml) lemon juice
3 egg yolks
1 cup cooked white short-grain rice

MERINGUE
3 egg whites
½ cup (110g) caster sugar

Process biscuits and rice cakes until finely crushed. Combine biscuit mixture, coconut and butter in bowl, press over base and half way up side of 24cm springform tin. Refrigerate 30 minutes.

Pour filling over base, bake in moderate oven about 15 minutes or until just set; cool, refrigerate until cold. Top filling with meringue, bake pie in moderate oven about 5 minutes or until lightly browned.
Filling: Combine all ingredients in bowl; mix well.
Meringue: Beat egg whites in small bowl with electric mixer until soft peaks form, gradually add sugar, beat until dissolved between additions.

Serves 6 to 8.

■ Recipe, without meringue topping, can be prepared a day ahead.
■ Storage: Covered, in refrigerator.
■ Freeze: Not suitable.
■ Microwave: Not suitable.

PLUM AND HAZELNUT RICE STRUDEL

2 x 825g cans dark plums in syrup
4 strips orange rind
1 cinnamon stick
⅓ cup (65g) white short-grain rice
½ cup (100g) firmly packed brown sugar
⅓ cup (35g) packaged ground hazelnuts
1 teaspoon ground cinnamon
8 sheets fillo pastry
30g butter, melted

MAPLE CREAM
300ml thickened cream
1 tablespoon maple-flavoured syrup

Drain plums, reserve 1½ cups (375ml) syrup. Halve plums, discard stones. Pat plums dry on absorbent paper. Combine reserved syrup, rind, cinnamon stick and rice in medium pan, cover, cook over low heat, stirring occasionally, until liquid is absorbed and rice tender; cool.

Combine sugar, nuts and ground cinnamon in bowl. Add plums and quarter of the nut mixture to rice mixture. Reserve quarter of remaining nut mixture for topping. Layer pastry, brushing every second sheet with butter and sprinkling with some of the nut mixture.

Place plum mixture along longest edge of pastry, leaving 2cm border on each side. Roll pastry to enclose filling, tucking in ends. Brush top of strudel with butter, sprinkle with reserved nut mixture. Place strudel on greased oven tray, bake in moderate oven about 30 minutes or until brown. Serve with maple cream.
Maple Cream: Beat cream and maple syrup in small bowl with electric mixer until soft peaks form.

Serves 6.

■ Recipe best made just before serving.
■ Freeze: Not suitable.
■ Microwave: Not suitable.

From back: Lemon Meringue Rice Pie, Plum and Hazelnut Rice Strudel.

Plates from Morris Home & Garden Wares; tiles from Country Floors.

APRICOT RICE CONDE

1.25 litres (5 cups) milk
½ vanilla bean, split
1 cup (200g) white short-grain rice
½ cup (110g) sugar
½ cup (75g) dried apricots, sliced
2 teaspoons gelatine
1 tablespoon water
½ cup (125ml) cream

RASPBERRY SAUCE
200g raspberries
2 tablespoons icing sugar mixture
1 tablespoon Cassis

Grease ring mould (1.5 litre/6 cup capacity). Combine milk, vanilla bean and rice in large heavy-based pan, cook, uncovered, over low heat about 30 minutes, stirring occasionally, or until rice is tender and mixture thickened. Remove vanilla bean. Stir in sugar and apricots; cool.

Sprinkle gelatine over water in cup, stand in small pan of simmering water, stir until gelatine is dissolved. Fold gelatine mixture into rice mixture. Beat cream in small bowl until firm peaks form, fold cream into rice mixture. Spoon mixture into prepared mould, cover, refrigerate until set. Turn onto serving plates, serve with raspberry sauce.

Raspberry Sauce: Push raspberries through a fine sieve, stir in sifted icing sugar and liqueur.

Serves 6 to 8.

■ Recipe best made a day ahead.
■ Storage: Covered, in refrigerator.
■ Freeze: Not suitable.
■ Microwave: Gelatine suitable.

CREAMY BLACK RICE

2 cups (400g) black glutinous rice
2 cups (500ml) cream
1 cup (250ml) milk
1 vanilla bean
¼ cup (60ml) Kahlua or Tia Maria

Place rice in bowl, cover well with water, cover, stand 12 hours; drain rice. Repeat this process twice more.

Add rice to pan of boiling water, simmer, uncovered, 15 minutes; drain. Combine rice with remaining ingredients in medium pan, simmer, uncovered, stirring occasionally, about 25 minutes or until liquid is almost absorbed and rice tender. Remove vanilla bean.

Serves 4 to 6.

- ■ Recipe best cooked just before serving.
- ■ Freeze: Not suitable.
- ■ Microwave: Suitable.

RICH CHOCOLATE FUDGE CAKE

250g dark chocolate, chopped
150g butter, chopped
3 eggs, separated
⅓ cup (65g) firmly packed brown sugar
¼ cup (60ml) Kahlua or Tia Maria
½ cup (60g) packaged ground almonds
½ cup (75g) rice flour

Grease deep 20cm round cake pan, cover base with baking paper, grease paper. Combine chocolate and butter in medium bowl over pan of simmering water, stir until melted; cool.

Beat egg yolks and sugar in small bowl with electric mixer until thick and creamy, stir in liqueur. Transfer mixture to large bowl, stir in chocolate mixture. Fold in nuts and flour.

Beat egg whites in small bowl with electric mixer until soft peaks form, fold into chocolate mixture in 2 batches. Pour mixture into prepared pan. Bake in moderately slow oven about 55 minutes or until firm; cool in pan. Serve cake dusted with sifted icing sugar, if desired.

- ■ Cake can be made 2 days ahead.
- ■ Storage: Covered, in refrigerator.
- ■ Freeze: Suitable.
- ■ Microwave: Chocolate and butter suitable.

ABOVE: From left: Apricot Rice Conde, Creamy Black Rice.
RIGHT: Rich Chocolate Fudge Cake.

Right: Tea-towel background from Morris Home & Garden Wares.

HAZELNUT AND CARAMEL RICE ICE-CREAM

3 cups (750ml) milk
1/4 cup (50g) white short-grain rice
1/3 cup (75g) caster sugar
2 egg yolks
300ml cream

CARAMEL
200g Jersey caramels, finely chopped
1 1/2 tablespoons water
1/3 cup (40g) toasted chopped
  hazelnuts

Heat milk in medium heavy-based pan, add rice, cook, uncovered, over low heat, stirring occasionally, about 50 minutes or until rice is very soft and mixture thickened; cool 10 minutes. Stir in sugar, yolks and cream. Pour rice mixture into 14cm x 21cm loaf pan, cover, freeze until just firm.

Transfer ice-cream to large bowl, beat with electric mixer until smooth, beat in caramel. Return mixture to pan, cover, freeze until firm. Serve with fruit, if desired.
Caramel: Combine caramels, water and nuts in small heavy-based pan, stir over very low heat until caramels are just melted; cool.

Serves 4.

- Recipe can be made 3 days ahead.
- Storage: Covered, in freezer.
- Microwave: Not suitable.

DEEP-FRIED STICKY RICE ICE-CREAM BALLS

1 litre vanilla ice-cream
300ml thickened cream
3/4 cup (180ml) milk
1 tablespoon caster sugar
2/3 cup (130g) arborio rice
1/2 cup (75g) finely chopped toasted
  macadamias
1/2 cup (35g) shredded coconut
1 egg, lightly beaten
vegetable oil for deep-frying

CHOCOLATE SAUCE
1 3/4 cups (430ml) milk
125g dark chocolate, chopped

Shape rounded tablespoons of ice-cream into balls. You will need 8 ice-cream balls for this recipe. Place ice-cream balls on tray, cover, freeze until firm.

Combine cream, milk and sugar in medium pan, bring to boil, add rice, simmer, partly covered, over very low heat about 15 minutes or until rice is tender and almost all the liquid is absorbed; stand, covered, 15 minutes. Stir in nuts, coconut and egg; cool.

Divide rice mixture into 8 portions, coat each ice-cream ball with rice mixture, return to tray, cover, freeze 1 hour.

Deep-fry rice balls in batches in hot oil until just browned, drain on absorbent paper. Serve immediately with chocolate sauce.
Chocolate Sauce: Bring milk to boil in pan, remove from heat, add chocolate, stir until chocolate is melted and mixture is well combined.

Serves 4.

- Uncooked rice balls can be made 2 days ahead.
- Storage: Covered, in freezer.
- Microwave: Chocolate sauce suitable.

From left: Deep-Fried Sticky Rice Ice-Cream Balls, Hazelnut and Caramel Rice Ice-Cream.

Stainless steel pourer from The Bay Tree Kitchen Shop.

CREAMY CHOCOLATE RICE TURNOVERS

40g butter
1 cup (100g) arborio rice
⅓ cup (80ml) creme de cacao
1½ cups (375ml) cream
2¼ cups (560ml) milk
50g dark chocolate, chopped
16 sheets fillo pastry
100g butter, melted, extra
½ cup (25g) flaked coconut

BRANDY CREME ANGLAISE
1½ cups (375ml) milk
½ cup (125ml) cream
1 vanilla bean, split
5 egg yolks
¼ cup (55g) caster sugar
¼ cup (60ml) brandy

Heat butter in pan, add rice and liqueur, cook, stirring, until liqueur is absorbed. Combine cream and milk in another pan, bring to boil, keep hot.

Stir ⅔ cup (160ml) hot milk mixture into rice mixture, cook, stirring, over low heat until liquid is absorbed. Continue adding milk mixture gradually, stirring until absorbed, before next addition. Total cooking time should be about 30 minutes or until rice is tender. Add chocolate, stir until melted; cool.

Divide mixture into 8 portions. Brush 2 sheets of pastry with some of the extra butter, fold in half lengthways, place a portion of rice mixture at 1 end. Fold corner of pastry diagonally across filling to form a triangle. Continue folding to end of strip, retaining triangular shape. Brush with a little more extra butter. Repeat with remaining pastry, extra butter and filling.

Place turnovers on greased oven tray, sprinkle with coconut. Bake in moderately hot oven about 10 minutes or until lightly browned and crisp. Serve warm, dusted with sifted icing sugar, if desired, and brandy creme anglaise.

Brandy Creme Anglaise: Combine milk, cream and vanilla bean in small pan, bring to boil, remove from heat, stand, covered, 20 minutes. Combine egg yolks, sugar and brandy in bowl; whisk until smooth. Gradually whisk milk mixture into egg mixture. Return mixture to pan, stir over low heat, without boiling, until mixture thickens slightly; strain.

Serves 8.

■ Recipe can be prepared a day ahead.
■ Storage: Covered, separately, in refrigerator.
■ Freeze: Uncooked turnovers suitable.
■ Microwave: Not suitable.

APPLE RICE TART WITH BUTTERSCOTCH SAUCE

2 cups cooked white long-grain rice
2 tablespoons caster sugar
1 tablespoon custard powder
2 eggs, lightly beaten
410g can pie apples
1 teaspoon ground cinnamon
1 teaspoon mixed spice
1 teaspoon grated lemon rind
½ cup (125ml) cream

BUTTERSCOTCH SAUCE
½ cup (100g) firmly packed
   brown sugar
60g unsalted butter, chopped
½ cup (125ml) cream

Grease 23cm shallow pie dish. Combine all ingredients in bowl, mix well; pour into prepared dish. Bake in moderately slow oven about 1¼ hours or until just set. Serve tart at room temperature, dusted with sifted icing sugar, if desired, and hot butterscotch sauce.

Butterscotch Sauce: Combine all ingredients in small heavy-based pan, stir over heat until butter is melted, boil, uncovered, 1 minute or until slightly thickened.

Serves 6.

■ Recipe can be made a day ahead.
■ Storage: Covered, separately,
   in refrigerator.
■ Freeze: Not suitable.
■ Microwave: Not suitable.

RHUBARB AND APPLE COBBLER

2 medium (300g) apples,
   peeled, sliced
5 cups (550g) chopped fresh rhubarb
½ cup (110g) caster sugar
¼ cup (60ml) apple juice
½ teaspoon ground cinnamon
½ cup (75g) self-raising flour
⅓ cup (50g) rice flour
⅓ cup (40g) packaged ground
   almonds
2 tablespoons brown sugar
¼ cup (60ml) sour cream
2 tablespoons flaked almonds

Combine apples, rhubarb, caster sugar and juice in pan, stir over heat, without boiling, until sugar is dissolved; simmer, covered, about 10 minutes or until apples are tender. Spread mixture into shallow ovenproof dish (1 litre/4 cup capacity).

Process cinnamon, flours, ground nuts, brown sugar and cream until mixture forms a ball. Knead dough lightly on floured surface, roll until 6mm thick. Cut pastry into 5cm shapes, overlap shapes on rhubarb mixture, sprinkle with flaked almonds. Bake in moderate oven about 40 minutes or until browned.

Serves 4 to 6.

■ Recipe best made close to serving.
■ Freeze: Not suitable.
■ Microwave: Apple mixture suitable.

LEFT: From left: Apple Rice Tart with Butterscotch Sauce, Rhubarb and Apple Cobbler.
BELOW: Creamy Chocolate Rice Turnovers.

OLD-FASHIONED CREAMED RICE

2 cups (500ml) milk
2 cups (500ml) cream
⅓ cup (75g) caster sugar
1 vanilla bean
¾ cup (150g) white short-grain rice

Combine milk, cream, sugar and vanilla bean in medium pan, bring to boil, stirring. Gradually stir in rice, cover pan tightly, cook over low heat, stirring occasionally, about 50 minutes or until rice is tender and most of the liquid is absorbed. Remove vanilla bean.

Serves 4.

■ Recipe best made just before serving.
■ Freeze: Not suitable.
■ Microwave: Suitable.

BROWN SUGAR RICE PUDDING

½ cup (100g) white short-grain rice
2 cups (500ml) milk
1 cup (250ml) cream
¼ cup (50g) brown sugar
1 tablespoon maple-flavoured syrup

Grease ovenproof dish (1 litre/4 cup capacity). Combine all ingredients in prepared dish, mix lightly with a fork. Bake, uncovered, in moderately slow oven about 1¾ hours or until most of the liquid has been absorbed.

Serves 4.

■ Recipe can be made a day ahead.
■ Storage: Covered, in refrigerator.
■ Freeze: Not suitable.
■ Microwave: Not suitable.

CREAMY BAKED RICE CUSTARD

4 eggs
⅓ cup (75g) caster sugar
1 teaspoon vanilla essence
2 cups (500ml) milk
300ml cream
⅓ cup (55g) sultanas
1½ cups cooked white short-grain rice
ground cinnamon

Whisk eggs, sugar and essence together in bowl. Gradually whisk milk and cream into egg mixture. Stir in sultanas and rice. Pour mixture into greased ovenproof dish (1.5 litre/6 cup capacity), place in baking dish with enough boiling water to come halfway up side of ovenproof dish. Bake, uncovered, in moderate oven 30 minutes,

ORANGE BUTTERMILK PANCAKES

¾ cup (105g) self-raising flour
½ cup (75g) rice flour
¼ cup (35g) buckwheat flour
⅓ cup (50g) shelled chopped pistachios, toasted
1¼ cups (310ml) buttermilk
60g butter, melted
½ cup (125ml) golden syrup
2 teaspoons grated orange rind
¼ cup (60ml) orange juice

LIQUEUR FRUITS
½ cup (125ml) water
¼ cup (55g) caster sugar
¼ cup (60ml) lime juice
1 tablespoon Grand Marnier
2kg piece of watermelon
250g strawberries, halved
200g blueberries

Sift flours into bowl, add nuts, gradually stir in combined buttermilk, butter, golden syrup, rind and juice; mix, blend or process until mixture is smooth. Grease heated heavy-based pan with a little extra butter, pour about ¼ cup batter evenly into pan. Cook pancake on both sides until lightly browned. Repeat with remaining batter. You need 12 pancakes for this recipe. Serve pancakes with liqueur fruits.

Liqueur Fruits: Combine water and sugar in pan, stir over heat, without boiling, until sugar is dissolved. Simmer, uncovered, about 8 minutes or until syrup is slightly thickened. Stir in juice and liqueur; cool.

Using a melon baller, scoop flesh from melon (you will need about 2 cups watermelon balls). Combine syrup, watermelon and berries in bowl, cover, refrigerate several hours.

Serves 6.

■ Pancakes best made close to serving. Liqueur fruits can be made a day ahead.
■ Storage: Covered, in refrigerator.
■ Freeze: Pancakes suitable.
■ Microwave: Not suitable.

...tir gently halfway by slipping a fork under ...e skin to distribute rice and sultanas ...venly through custard. Dust with cin-...amon, bake further 15 minutes or until ...ustard is firm.

...erves 6.

■ Recipe can be made a day ahead.
■ Storage: Covered, in refrigerator.
■ Freeze: Not suitable.
■ Microwave: Not suitable.

...BOVE: Clockwise from top left: Brown ...ugar Rice Pudding, Creamy Baked Rice ...ustard, Old-Fashioned Creamed Rice. ...IGHT: Orange Buttermilk Pancakes.

...bove: Colander from Pacific East India Company.

ITALIAN RICE CREAM

2 tablespoons arborio rice
⅓ cup (75g) caster sugar
1½ cups (375ml) hot milk
2 teaspoons gelatine
1 tablespoon water
½ cup (125ml) cream
1 tablespoon finely chopped
　　glace figs
1 tablespoon chopped mixed peel
2 tablespoons finely chopped
　　glace apricots
1 cup (250g) mascarpone cheese

PEACH AMARETTO PUREE
2 medium (400g) peaches,
　　peeled, seeded
2 tablespoons Amaretto
1 tablespoon caster sugar

Grease 4 moulds (¾ cup/180ml capacity).
Combine rice, sugar and ¼ cup (60ml) of
the hot milk in small heavy-based pan, stir
over heat until milk is absorbed. Continue
adding milk ¼ cup at a time, stirring until
absorbed before each addition. Total
cooking time should be about 20 minutes
or until rice is tender; cool 10 minutes.

Sprinkle gelatine over water in cup,
stand in small pan of simmering water, stir
until dissolved. Beat cream in small bowl
until soft peaks form. Stir gelatine mixture,
cream and remaining ingredients into rice
mixture. Divide mixture between prepared
moulds, cover, refrigerate until set. Turn
onto serving plates, serve with peach
Amaretto puree.
Peach Amaretto Puree: Blend or
process all ingredients until smooth.

Serves 4.

■ Recipe can be made a day ahead.
■ Storage: Covered, separately,
　in refrigerator.
■ Freeze: Not suitable.
■ Microwave: Gelatine suitable.

CRISPY GLUTINOUS RICE TRIANGLES

2 cups (400g) white glutinous rice
2 cups (500ml) water
½ teaspoon rosewater
vegetable oil for deep-frying
¼ cup (55g) caster sugar
½ teaspoon ground cinnamon
pinch ground cardamom

Place rice in bowl, cover well with water,
cover, stand overnight.

Grease 19cm x 29cm rectangular slice
pan. Drain rice, combine with the 2 cups
of water in medium heavy-based pan,
bring to boil, reduce heat, simmer,
covered, about 40 minutes or until liquid
is absorbed and rice tender. Stir in
rosewater. Press rice firmly into prepared
pan, refrigerate until cold.

Turn rice onto board, cut into triangles.
Deep-fry triangles in batches in hot oil
until crisp and browned, toss in combined sugar, cinnamon and cardamom.
Serve warm.

Serves 6 to 8.

■ Recipe can be prepared a day ahead.
■ Storage: Covered, in refrigerator.
■ Freeze: Not suitable.
■ Microwave: Not suitable.

HAZELNUT PRALINE PANCAKES

¾ cup (105g) self-raising flour
¼ cup (25g) packaged ground
　　hazelnuts
1 tablespoon brown sugar
¾ cup cooked white short-grain rice
2 eggs, separated
¾ cup (180ml) milk
25g unsalted butter, melted
2 tablespoons Frangelico
125g unsalted butter, extra

MAPLE SAUCE
100g unsalted butter
½ cup (100g) firmly packed brown sugar
½ cup (125ml) water
½ cup (125ml) maple-flavoured syrup

PRALINE
1 cup (220g) caster sugar
1 cup (250ml) water
¾ cup (105g) roasted hazelnuts

POLENTA STARS IN ORANGE SYRUP

½ cup (80g) chopped seedless dates
½ cup (75g) chopped dried apricots
1 tablespoon finely chopped
   glace ginger
2 tablespoons Cointreau
½ cup (100g) white short-grain rice
3 cups (750ml) milk
300ml cream
⅓ cup (65g) firmly packed
   brown sugar
2 tablespoons orange marmalade
½ cup (85g) polenta
½ cup (60g) chopped toasted walnuts
plain flour
2 eggs, lightly beaten
polenta, extra
vegetable oil for deep-frying
⅓ cup (75g) caster sugar

ORANGE SYRUP
3 strips orange rind
1 cup (250ml) orange juice
⅓ cup (80ml) maple-flavoured syrup
2 tablespoons caster sugar
1 tablespoon Cointreau

Grease 26cm x 32cm Swiss roll pan, line base and 2 opposite sides of pan with baking paper. Combine dates, apricots, ginger and liqueur in bowl.

Combine rice, milk, cream, brown sugar and marmalade in large pan, stir over low heat until sugar is dissolved. Bring to boil, add polenta, simmer, uncovered, about 15 minutes or until rice is tender, stirring occasionally. Stir in date mixture and nuts. Spread mixture into prepared pan, cover, refrigerate 3 hours or until firm.

Cut mixture into 7cm star shapes. Toss stars in flour, shake away excess flour, then dip in eggs and extra polenta. Deep-fry stars in hot oil until lightly browned; drain on absorbent paper. Toss stars in caster sugar, serve with orange syrup.

Orange Syrup: Cut rind into strips. Combine rind, juice, maple syrup and sugar in small pan, stir over low heat until sugar is dissolved. Simmer, uncovered, without stirring, about 10 minutes or until slightly thickened. Stir in liqueur.

Serves 4 to 6.

■ Polenta stars and orange syrup can be made a day ahead.
■ Storage: Covered, in refrigerator.
■ Freeze: Not suitable.
■ Microwave: Not suitable.

Sift flour and ground nuts into medium bowl, stir in sugar and rice. Gradually stir in combined egg yolks, milk, melted butter and liqueur; cover, refrigerate 30 minutes.

Beat egg whites until soft peaks form, fold into batter. Drop ⅓ cup (80ml) of mixture into heated greased heavy-based pan, spread into a 10cm round, cook until pancake is browned underneath and bubbles appear. Turn to brown other side. Repeat with remaining batter. You need 8 pancakes for this recipe.

Beat extra butter in small bowl with electric mixer until light and fluffy. Serve pancakes with whipped butter, maple sauce and praline.

Maple Sauce: Heat butter, sugar, water and maple syrup in small pan, stir over low heat until sugar is dissolved, simmer, uncovered, without stirring, about 15 minutes or until slightly thickened.

Praline: Combine sugar and water in small pan, stir over heat, without boiling, until sugar is dissolved. Boil, uncovered, without stirring, until mixture is golden brown. Place nuts on oiled oven tray, pour hot toffee over nuts; cool. Break into pieces when cold.

Serves 8.

■ Pancakes and whipped butter best made just before serving. Maple sauce can be made a day ahead.
■ Storage: Maple sauce, covered, at room temperature.
■ Freeze: Pancakes suitable.
■ Microwave: Not suitable.

LEFT: Italian Rice Cream.
ABOVE: Clockwise from left: Hazelnut Praline Pancakes, Crispy Glutinous Rice Triangles, Polenta Stars in Orange Syrup.

Above: Setting from House.

119

Nutritionists today believe that rice is more important to our health and energy than we realised. Often called the "grain of life", rice is one of the oldest and most cultivated cereal grains. It is high in complex carbohydrates – great for energy – and has virtually no fat, sugar or salt. Half a cup of cooked rice supplies about 350 kilojoules (85 calories), which is equivalent to a thick slice of bread.

Current research indicates that cooked rice, whether white or brown, also contains what is called resistant starch. This means it resists digestion, and produces a healthy environment in the colon. Resistant starch is now believed to be as important as fibre in your diet.

All rice is good for you, but brown rice – particularly if you are a vegetarian – is more nutritious than white rice because the bran layer is still intact. The bran layer is high in dietary fibre and B-group vitamins, plus important minerals including potassium, phosphorus, magnesium and zinc.

The bran layer in brown rice is a rich source of both poly- and mono-unsaturated oils and the powerful anti-oxidant Vitamin E. Rice bran oil, found in brown rice, has been shown to help lower blood cholesterol levels. The bran layer is also a rich source of insoluble fibre, a useful laxative.

We used both white and brown rice in our recipes, and specified short-grain (also known commercially as medium-grain) or long-grain for white rice. Some recipes use wild rice; this is not a true rice, but an aquatic grass, with similar cooking properties to brown rice.

Rice is the least allergy-producing grain, making it ideal for many people with allergies or food intolerances. It is easy to digest and, because rice is gluten free, it is the major cereal grain for people with coeliac disease – a sensitivity to gluten, the protein in wheat and other cereals.

HELPFUL TIPS

- 1 cup of uncooked brown or white rice = 200g.
- 1 cup of uncooked wild rice = 180g.
- White rice almost triples in bulk during cooking, while brown and wild rice double in bulk.
- There is no need to wash Australian-grown rice for cleanliness.
- Store uncooked rice, tightly covered, in a cool, dark place. Check the "use by" date for a guide to keeping times.
- Left-over cooked rice can be stored, covered, in the refrigerator for up to 2 days or frozen, securely wrapped, for up to 2 months.
- Quick-cook rice and ready-cooked frozen rice are convenient products when you are in a hurry; look for them in your supermarket.
- We have not included salt in our recipes; use salt to personal taste.

COOKING AND REHEATING RICE

COOKING RICE

ABSORPTION (STEAMED) METHOD

Combine water and rice in medium heavy-based pan, cover tightly, bring to boil, reduce heat to as low as possible, cook for recommended time. Do not remove lid during cooking time. Remove pan from heat, stand, covered, 10 minutes. Fluff rice with a fork.

MICROWAVE METHOD

Combine rice and boiling water in large microwave-safe bowl or jug. Cook, uncovered, on HIGH for recommended time or until rice is tender. Stir halfway through cooking. Cover, stand 5 minutes. Fluff rice with a fork.

BAKED METHOD

Combine rice and boiling water in ovenproof dish, stir well. Cover tightly with foil or lid. Bake in moderate oven for recommended time or until rice is tender. Fluff rice with a fork.

BOILED METHOD

Bring water to boil in large pan, add rice, stir to separate grains, boil, uncovered, for recommended time or until rice is tender; drain.

An electric rice cooker or a rice steamer will also give good, consistent results. The choice is a matter of personal preference. Do not rinse cooked rice unless specified in recipes.

COOKING TIMES FOR RICE   NOTE: we used an 830 watt microwave oven

WHITE RICE (LONG- AND SHORT-GRAIN)

METHOD	QUANTITY OF RICE	QUANTITY OF WATER	COOKING TIME
ABSORPTION	1½ cups (300g)	3 cups/750ml	10 minutes
MICROWAVE	1½ cups (300g)	3 cups/750ml	10 minutes
BAKED	1½ cups (300g)	2½ cups/625ml	25 minutes
BOILED	1½ cups (300g)	8 cups/2 litres	12 minutes

BROWN RICE (LONG- AND SHORT-GRAIN)

METHOD	QUANTITY OF RICE	QUANTITY OF WATER	COOKING TIME
ABSORPTION	1½ cups (300g)	3½ cups/875ml	30 minutes
MICROWAVE	1½ cups (300g)	3½ cups/875ml	25 minutes
BAKED	1½ cups (300g)	3½ cups/875ml	1 hour
BOILED	1½ cups (300g)	8 cups/2 litres	25 minutes

WILD RICE

METHOD	QUANTITY OF RICE	QUANTITY OF WATER	COOKING TIME
ABSORPTION	½ cup (90g)	1½ cups/375ml	40 minutes
MICROWAVE	½ cup (90g)	2 cups/500ml	25 minutes
BAKED	½ cup (90g)	½ cup/125ml	30 minutes
BOILED	½ cup (90g)	4 cups/l litre	20 minutes

REHEATING COOKED RICE

Reheating time will depend on the temperature and quantity of the rice.

- Place rice in colander, stand over pan of simmering water; cover, heat.
- Add just enough water to a frying pan to barely cover base. Bring to the boil, add rice, cover, heat until water is absorbed.
- Spread rice into greased, shallow oven-proof dish, sprinkle with a little water or milk, dot with butter. Cover, heat in moderate oven.
- Heat a little butter or oil in a wok or frying pan, add rice, stir gently with a fork until hot.
- Place rice in microwave-safe dish, cover, heat on HIGH.

·Glossary·

Here are some terms, names and alternatives to help everyone use and understand our recipes perfectly.

ALLSPICE: pimento.

AMARETTO: almond-flavoured liqueur.

BACON RASHERS: bacon slices.

BAKING POWDER (double-acting baking powder): a raising agent consisting of a starch, but mostly cream of tartar and bicarbonate of soda in the proportions of 1 level teaspoon cream of tartar to ½ level teaspoon bicarbonate of soda. This is equivalent to 2 teaspoons of baking powder.

BEAN SPROUTS:

Bean sprouts

Mung bean sprouts

BEEF:

Blade steak: the very large shoulder area consisting of a variety of muscles.

Chuck steak: comes from the upper shoulder and neck area consisting of many small muscles joined by connective tissue.

Eye-fillet: tenderloin.

Minced: ground beef.

Rump steak: boneless piece of meat that covers the hip bone.

Scotch fillet: eye of the rib roast; rib-eye roll; cube roll.

BELACAN: also known as belachan and blachan. Dried shrimp paste, it is sold in slabs or flat cakes. There is no real substitute; however, shrimp paste could be used.

Belacan

Shrimp paste

BICARBONATE OF SODA: baking soda.

BREADCRUMBS:

Packaged: use fine packaged breadcrumbs.

Stale: use 1- or 2-day-old bread made into crumbs by grating, blending or processing.

BUTTER: use salted or unsalted (also called sweet) butter; 125g is equal to 1 stick butter.

BUTTERMILK: is now made by adding a culture to skim milk to give a slightly acidic flavour; skim milk can be substituted, if preferred.

CAJUN SEASONING: a combination of dried ingredients consisting of salt, blended peppers, garlic, onion and spices.

CALAMARI: a type of squid.

CASSIS: blackcurrant-flavoured liqueur.

CHEESE:

Blue vein: we used a firm blue cheese.

Bocconcini: small balls of mild, delicate cheese packaged in water or whey to keep them white and soft. The water should be just milky in appearance and cheese should be white; yellowing indicates that it is too old.

Cream: also known as Philly.

Feta: a soft Greek cheese with a sharp, salty taste.

Mascarpone: a fresh, unripened smooth triple cream cheese with a rich sweet taste, slightly acidic.

Mozzarella: a fresh, semi-soft cheese with a delicate, clean, fresh curd taste; it has a low melting point and stringy texture when heated.

Parmesan: sharp-tasting hard cheese used as a flavour accent. We prefer to use fresh parmesan cheese, although it is available already finely grated.

Ricotta: a fresh, unripened light curd cheese.

Romano: hard cheese, straw coloured with a grainy texture and sharp, tangy flavour. Good for grating.

Smoked: use a firm smoked cheese.

Tasty cheddar: matured cheddar; use a hard, good-tasting variety.

CHICKPEAS: also known as ceci and garbanzos.

CHILLIES: available in many different types and sizes. Use rubber gloves when chopping fresh chillies as they can burn your skin. Keep hands away from your eyes and face.

Crushed, dried: available from supermarkets and Asian food stores.

Powder: the Asian variety is the hottest and is made from ground chillies; it can be used as a substitute for fresh chillies in the proportions of ½ teaspoon ground chilli powder to 1 medium chopped fresh chilli.

Sweet chilli sauce: we used a mild sauce made from red chillies, sugar, garlic, salt and vinegar.

CHINESE BARBECUED PORK: roasted pork fillets available from many Asian food and specialty stores.

CHORIZO SAUSAGE: spicy sausage made with pork.

COCONUT: use desiccated coconut unless otherwise specified.

Cream: available in cans and cartons.

Flaked: flaked dried coconut flesh.

Milk: available in cans.

Shredded: thin strips of dried coconut.

COINTREAU: orange-flavoured liqueur.

CONDENSED MILK: we used Nestle's milk which has had 60 per cent of the water removed, then sweetened with sugar.

CONSOMME: thin, clear soup.

COOKING OIL SPRAY: available in spray cans. Different types are available; you can use any of them.

CORNFLOUR: cornstarch.

CREAM: fresh pouring cream; has a minimum fat content of 35 per cent.

Sour: a thick, commercially cultured soured cream.

Sour light: a less dense, commercially cultured soured cream; it will not set as firmly as sour cream.

Thickened (whipping): is specified when necessary in recipes. Double cream or cream with more than 35 per cent fat can be substituted.

CREME DE CACAO: chocolate-flavoured liqueur.

CSABAI: Hungarian sausage made from pork, seasoned with paprika and well smoked.

CURRY PASTE: we used bottled curry pastes, available from supermarkets and Asian specialty stores.

Green: consisting of red onion, green chilli, soy bean oil, garlic, galangal, lemon grass, shrimp paste, citrus peel, salt, coriander seed and citric acid.

Madras: consisting of coriander, cumin, pepper, turmeric, chilli, garlic, ginger, vinegar and oil.

Tikka: consisting of chilli, coriander, cumin, lentil flour, garlic, ginger, oil, turmeric, fennel, pepper, cloves, cinnamon and cardamom.

Vindaloo: a fiery hot/sour flavour consisting of coriander, cumin, turmeric, chilli, ginger, garlic, tamarind, lentil flour and spices.

CURRY POWDER: consisting of chilli, coriander, cumin, fennel, fenugreek and turmeric.

CUSTARD POWDER: also known as vanilla pudding mix.

EGGPLANT: aubergine.

ESSENCE: extract.

FILLO PASTRY: also known as phyllo dough; comes in tissue-thin pastry sheets bought chilled or frozen.

FISH SAUCE: made from the liquid drained from salted, fermented anchovies. It has a strong smell and taste; use sparingly. There are several varieties available in different strengths and flavours.

FIVE SPICE POWDER: a pungent mixture of ground spices which include cinnamon, cloves, fennel, star anise and Szechuan peppers.

FLOUR:

Brown rice: flour made from ground wholegrain rice.

Buckwheat: flour milled from buckwheat.

Gluten: has a high protein content and is used in commercial bread making. It is available from health food stores.

Plain: all-purpose flour.

Rice: flour made from polished rice, very finely ground. Ground rice is similar to rice flour, but coarser in texture. The two are interchangeable.

Rye: flour milled from rye.

Self-raising: substitute plain (all-purpose) flour and baking powder in the proportions of 1 cup (150g) plain flour to 2 level teaspoons baking powder. Sift together several times before using.

Soya: a strong-flavoured flour processed from soya beans.

Wholemeal plain: wholewheat flour without the addition of baking powder.

FRANGELICO: hazelnut-flavoured liqueur.

GARAM MASALA: often used in Indian cooking, this spice combines cardamom, cinnamon, cloves, coriander, cumin and nutmeg in varying proportions. Sometimes pepper is used to make a hot variation.

GELATINE: we used unflavoured powdered gelatine.

GHEE: a pure butter fat, it can be heated to high temperatures without burning because of the lack of salts and milk solids.

GOLDEN SYRUP: a golden-coloured syrup made from sugar cane. Maple syrup, pancake syrup or honey can be substituted.

GRAND MARNIER: orange-flavoured liqueur.

HERBS:

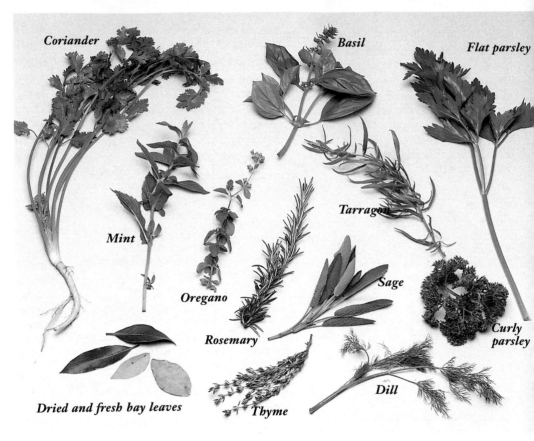

Coriander Basil Flat parsley Mint Tarragon Oregano Sage Rosemary Curly parsley Dried and fresh bay leaves Thyme Dill

HOI SIN SAUCE: a thick, sweet, Chinese barbecue sauce made from salted black beans, onion and garlic.

ITALIAN SAUSAGES: large, fresh, lightly salted pork sausages.

JALAPENO PEPPERS: hot chillies, available bottled or canned in brine.

JERSEY CARAMELS: made from sugar, glucose, condensed milk, flour, oil and gelatine.

KAHLUA: coffee-flavoured liqueur.

LAMB:

Diced: cubed.

Fillet: tenderloin; the smaller piece of meat from a row of loin chops or cutlets.

Minced: ground lamb.

Neck chops: cut from the section where the neck joins the forequarter.

LAMB:

Shank: portion of front or back leg with bone in.

Shoulder: can be bought with or without the bone.

LARD: fat obtained from melting down and clarifying pork fat; available packaged.

LENTILS: dried pulses.

MAPLE-FLAVOURED SYRUP: golden syrup, pancake syrup or honey can be substituted.

MILK: we used full-cream milk unless otherwise specified.

MIXED SPICE: a blend of ground spices usually consisting of cinnamon, allspice and nutmeg.

MORTADELLA: a delicately spiced and smoked cooked sausage made from pork and beef.

MUD CRAB: mangrove crab.

MUSHROOMS:

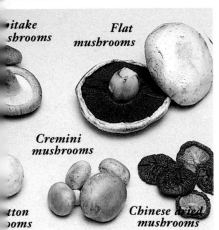

itake shrooms
Flat mushrooms
Cremini mushrooms
tton ooms
Chinese dried mushrooms

NUTS:

OIL:

Extra virgin: the highest quality oil, obtained from the first olive pressings.

Olive: a blend of refined and virgin olive oils; good for everyday cooking.

Peanut: made from ground peanuts, is commonly used in Asian cooking; a lighter salad type of oil can be used.

Sesame: an oil made from roasted, crushed white sesame seeds. Do not use for deep- or shallow-frying.

Vegetable: we used a polyunsaturated vegetable oil.

ORANGE FLOWER WATER: concentrated flavouring made from orange blossoms.

OYSTER SAUCE: a rich brown sauce made from oysters cooked in salt and soy sauce, then thickened with starches.

PANCETTA: cured pork belly; bacon can be substituted.

PAPPADUMS: wafer-thin bread made from lentil flour and seasonings; it is available in packets from supermarkets. They can be deep-fried or cooked in a microwave oven.

PAPRIKA: ground dried peppers, available sweet or hot.

PEARL BARLEY: barley which has had most of its outer husk removed.

PEPPERONI: sausage made from minced pork and beef with added fat; flavoured with hot red pepper.

PESTO: a paste made from basil, oil, pine nuts, garlic and parmesan cheese.

POLENTA: usually made from ground corn (maize); similar to cornmeal but coarser and darker in colour. One can be substituted for the other but results will be slightly different.

PORK:

Fillet: skinless, boneless eye-fillet cut from the loin.

Minced: ground pork.

Neck: sometimes called pork scotch, from foreloin of pork.

Steaks: also known as schnitzels.

PRAWNS: shrimps.

PROSCIUTTO: uncooked, unsmoked ham cured in salt; ready to eat when bought.

PRUNES: whole dried plums.

READY-ROLLED PUFF PASTRY: frozen sheets of puff pastry available from supermarkets.

RHUBARB: a vegetable, the stalks of which are generally cooked and eaten as a fruit.

RICE PRODUCTS:

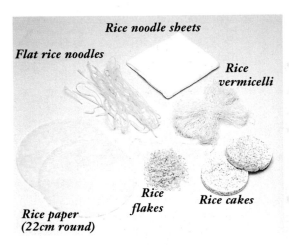

Rice noodle sheets
Flat rice noodles
Rice vermicelli
Rice flakes
Rice cakes
Rice paper (22cm round)

ROLLED OATS: oats have the husks ground off and are then steam-softened and rolled flat.

ROSEWATER: extract made from crushed rose petals.

SAFFRON: available in strands or ground form. The quality varies greatly.

SAMBAL OELEK: also ulek or olek, it is a paste made from chillies and salt.

SHALLOTS:

French: very small onion with brown skin. It grows in clusters, and has a strong onion and garlic flavour.

Green: also known as spring onions, scallions and eschallots.

SHRIMP PASTE: dark brown, strong-tasting flavouring made from salted dried shrimp.

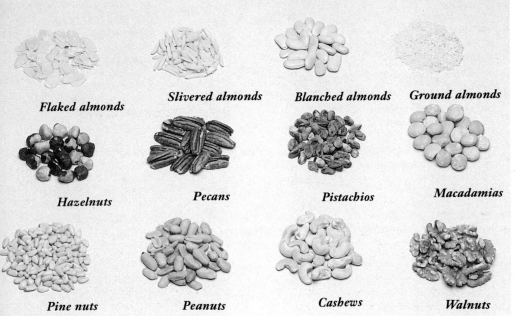

Flaked almonds
Slivered almonds
Blanched almonds
Ground almonds
Hazelnuts
Pecans
Pistachios
Macadamias
Pine nuts
Peanuts
Cashews
Walnuts

SILVERBEET:

Silverbeet

English spinach

SNOW PEAS: also known as mange tout (eat all).

SPATCHCOCKS: small chickens, weighing around 500g.

SUGAR: we used coarse granulated table sugar, also known as crystal sugar, unless otherwise specified.

Brown: a soft, fine granulated sugar containing molasses.

Caster: also known as superfine; is fine granulated table sugar.

Icing sugar mixture: also known as confectioners' sugar or powdered sugar. We used icing sugar mixture, not pure icing sugar, unless otherwise specified.

SZECHUAN PEPPER: also known as Chinese pepper; small red-brown

aromatic seeds resembling black peppercorns. They have a peppery lemon flavour. We used a convenient bottled combination of pepper, garlic, sugar and onion, available in Asian food stores and some supermarkets.

TACO SEASONING MIX: a convenient dry blend of cornflour, spices, chilli, salt and pepper.

TERIYAKI SAUCE: based on the lighter Japanese soy sauce; contains sugar, spices and vinegar.

TOMATO:

Paste: a concentrated tomato puree used in flavouring soups, stews, sauces and casseroles, etc.

Puree: is canned, pureed tomatoes (not tomato paste). Use fresh, peeled, pureed tomatoes as a substitute, if preferred.

Sauce: tomato ketchup.

Sun-dried: dried tomatoes, sometimes bottled in oil.

VEAL: the meat from a very young calf that can be identified by pale pink flesh.

Cutlets: from the neck end of the loin.

Diced: cubed.

Minced: ground veal.

VINEGAR: we used both white and brown malt vinegar.

Balsamic: originated in the province of Modena, Italy. Regional wine is specially processed then aged in antique wooden casks to give a pungent flavour.

Cider vinegar: vinegar made from fermented apples.

Red wine: based on red wine.

Rice: a colourless, seasoned vinegar containing sugar and salt.

White: made from spirit of cane sugar.

White wine: based on white wine.

WASABI PASTE: green horseradish.

YEAST: allow 2 teaspoons (7g) dried yeast to each 15g compressed yeast if substituting one for the other.

ZUCCHINI: courgette.

MAKE YOUR OWN STOCK

If you prefer to make your own stock, these recipes can be made up to 4 days ahead and stored, covered, in the refrigerator. Be sure to remove any fat from the surface after the cooled stock has been refrigerated overnight. If the stock is to be kept longer, it is best to freeze it in smaller quantities. Stock is also available in cans or tetra packs. Be aware of their salt content. Stock cubes or powder can be used. As a guide, 1 teaspoon of stock powder or 1 small crumbled stock cube mixed with 1 cup (250ml) water will give a fairly strong stock. Be aware of the salt and fat content of stock cubes and powders.

BEEF STOCK
2kg meaty beef bones
2 medium (300g) onions
2 sticks celery, chopped
2 medium (250g) carrots, chopped
3 bay leaves
2 teaspoons black peppercorns
5 litres (20 cups) water
3 litres (12 cups) water, extra

Place bones and unpeeled chopped onions in baking dish. Bake in hot oven about 1 hour or until bones and onions are well browned. Transfer bones and onions to large pan, add celery, carrots, bay leaves, peppercorns and water, simmer, uncovered, 3 hours. Add extra water, simmer, uncovered, further 1 hour; strain.

FISH STOCK
1.5kg fish bones
3 litres (12 cups) water
1 medium (150g) onion, chopped
2 sticks celery, chopped
2 bay leaves
1 teaspoon black peppercorns

Combine all ingredients in large pan, simmer, uncovered, 20 minutes; strain.

CHICKEN STOCK
2kg chicken bones
2 medium (300g) onions, chopped
2 sticks celery, chopped
2 medium (250g) carrots, chopped
3 bay leaves
2 teaspoons black peppercorns
5 litres (20 cups) water

Combine all ingredients in large pan, simmer, uncovered, 2 hours; strain.

VEGETABLE STOCK
2 large (360g) carrots, chopped
2 large (360g) parsnips, chopped
4 medium (600g) onions, chopped
12 sticks celery, chopped
4 bay leaves
2 teaspoons black peppercorns
6 litres (24 cups) water

Combine all ingredients in large pan, simmer, uncovered, 1½ hours; strain.

All stock recipes make about 2.5 litres (10 cups).

· Index ·

A

Anise Terrine with Summer Fruits 102
Apple Rice Tart with Butterscotch
   Sauce 115
Apricot Rice Conde 110
Artichoke Pizza with Red Pesto,
   Rice and 26
Asparagus Mushroom Salad with
   Rice Pesto 97
Avocado Roulade, Kumara and 19

B

Bacon, Bean and Rice Tacos 20
Bacon Fried Rice, Chicken and 65
Bacon Rice, Herb and 98
Bacon Rolls, Eggplant 9
Bacon Rolls, Veal and 56
Baked Rice and Ricotta Gnocchi 80
Baked Rice Custard, Creamy 116
Baked Risotto with Eggplants 57
Banana Rice Cake, Moist 105
Barbecued Pork Salad 91
Barley Country Soup, Rice and 15
Beef and Rice Noodles 76
Beef Casserole with Spicy Rice
   Dumplings 44
Beef, Mediterranean-Style 73
Beef Steak Pudding with Buttermilk
   Crust 30
Beef with Avocado Salsa, Creole-Style 69
Best-Ever Fried Rice 85
Biriani, Lamb 35
Biriani, Pork 62
Black Rice, Creamy 111
Braised Lamb Shanks in Spiced
   Tomato Sauce 38
Bread, Multigrain 12
Broad Beans and Red Pepper, Wild
   Rice with 97
Brown Sugar Rice Pudding 116
Brulee, Coffee Rice 105
Buttermilk Pancakes, Orange 117
Buttermilk Pikelets with Nutty Pepper
   Salsa 23
Butterscotch Souffles, Date and 106

C

Cake, Chocolate Pistachio Rice 100
Cake, Continental Rice 105
Cake, Moist Banana Rice 105
Cake, Rich Chocolate Fudge 111
Cake with Coffee Creme Anglaise,
   Double Nut 100
Cantonese-Style Deep-Fried Chicken 64
Caramel Rice Ice-Cream, Hazelnut
   and 112
Casserole, Cheesy Rice, Pepper and
   Eggplant 54
Casserole, Crunchy-Topped Sausage
   and Pepper 44
Casserole, Lamb, Rice and Almond 52
Casserole with Coriander Rice,
   Coconut 34
Casserole with Spicy Rice Dumplings,
   Beef 44
Cheese, Nut and Olive Bitelets 22
Cheese Tempters, Triple 24
Cheese Torte, Rice and 12

Cheesy Rice, Pepper and Eggplant
   Casserole 54
Chicken and Asparagus Pastries,
   Creamy 46
Chicken and Bacon Fried Rice 65
Chicken and Coconut Curry in
   Rice Nests 43
Chicken and Rice Salad, Smoked 6
Chicken and Seafood Paella 33
Chicken, Cantonese-Style Deep-Fried 64
Chicken, Indian Pilaf with Crunchy
   Marinated 31
Chicken Patties, Spicy Prawn and 64
Chicken Soup with Cheesy Rice
   Balls, Creamy 6
Chicken, Sweet 'n' Spicy Jamaican 70
Chicken with Cheesy Rice Topping,
   Oregano 50
Chicken with Salsa in Rice Cups, Spicy 20
Chickpea and Rice Ball Curry 40
Chickpeas and Rice, Curried 89
Chilli Crab and Prawn Combination Rice 71
Chilli Relish, Puffed Rice Crisps with 26
Chocolate Fudge Cake, Rich 111
Chocolate Pistachio Rice Cake 100
Chocolate Rice Turnovers, Creamy 114
Cobbler, Rhubarb and Apple 115
Coconut Lamb Casserole with
   Coriander Rice 34
Coconut Rice 98
Coffee Rice Brulee 105
Conde, Apricot Rice 110
Continental Rice Cake 105
Corn and Coriander Soup 5
Crab and Prawn Combination
   Rice, Chilli 71
Cream, Italian Rice 118
Creamed Rice, Old-Fashioned 116
Creamy Baked Rice Custard 116
Creamy Black Rice 111
Creamy Chicken and Asparagus
   Pastries 46
Creamy Chicken Soup with Cheesy
   Rice Balls 6
Creamy Chocolate Rice Turnovers 114
Creamy Seafood Rice Flans 72
Creole-Style Beef with Avocado Salsa 69
Crispy Glutinous Rice Triangles 118
Crunchy-Topped Sausage and
   Pepper Casserole 44
Curried Chickpeas and Rice 89
Curried Rice and Lentils with Fried
   Onions 40
Curried Rice Patties and Vegetable
   Stack 63
Curry, Chickpea and Rice Ball 40
Curry in Rice Nests, Chicken
   and Coconut 34
Curry Rice 83

D, E

Date and Butterscotch Souffles 106
Deep-Fried Sticky Rice Ice-Cream Balls 112
Double Nut Cake with Coffee Creme
   Anglaise 100
Double Rice Patties with Garlic
   Mayonnaise 18
Duck with Wild Rice and Orange
   Mustard Sauce 79
Eggplant Bacon Rolls 9
Eggplants, Baked Risotto with 57

F

Fennel Risotto, Kumara and 88
Fish and Rice Strudels, Smoked 47
Fish in Beer Batter with Tarragon
   Mayonnaise 67
Fried Rice Balls 41
Fried Rice, Best-Ever 85
Fried Rice, Chicken and Bacon 65
Fried Rice, Thai-Style 2
Frittata, Leek, Prosciutto and Rice 22
Frittata, Nutty Cheese and Rice 4
Fruit and Nut Veal Pilaf 46
Fruity Rice, Pork with 48

G, H

Gnocchi, Baked Rice and Ricotta 80
Gougere with Smoked Salmon
   Kedgeree Filling 49
Grilled Vegetable Flan 12
Gumbo with Seafood, Saffron Rice 75
Ham and Zucchini Muffins 15
Harissa Rice Salad, Roasted
   Vegetables with 61
Hashbrowns with Onion Tomato Relish 8
Hazelnut and Caramel Rice Ice-Cream 112
Hazelnut Praline Pancakes 118
Herb and Bacon Rice 98
Herbed Rice 93

I, J

Ice-Cream Balls, Deep-Fried
   Sticky Rice 112
Ice-Cream, Hazelnut and Caramel
   Rice 112
Indian Pilaf with Crunchy Marinated
   Chicken 31
Indian Rice 92
Indian Rice Pancake 89
Italian Rice Cream 118
Jambalaya 78
Jasmine Rice Salad with Chilli
   Coconut Dressing 90

K, L

Kedgeree Filling, Gougere with
   Smoked Salmon 49
Kumara and Avocado Roulade 19
Kumara and Fennel Risotto 88
Lamb and Red Pepper Rice Pastries 36
Lamb and Rice Noodle Lasagne 52
Lamb and Rice Pies 39
Lamb and Wild Rice Salad, Warm 36
Lamb Biriani 35
Lamb Casserole with Coriander
   Rice, Coconut 34
Lamb, Rice and Almond Casserole 52
Lamb Shanks in Spiced Tomato
   Sauce, Braised 38
Lasagne, Lamb and Rice Noodle 52
Layered Rice Cake 38
Leek, Prosciutto and Rice Frittata 22
Lemon Meringue Rice Pie 109
Lentils with Fried Onions, Curried
   Rice and 40

M

Meatballs, Pesto Risotto with 28
Meatballs, Spicy Minted 76
Meatloaf, Nutty Olive and Rice 75
Mediterranean-Style Beef........................... 73
Mexican-Style Rice 95
Mexican-Style Rice Pudding.................... 106
Middle Eastern Rice 93
Minestrone Soup with Rice Croutons,
   Spicy...6
Mocha Risotto.. 106
Moist Banana Rice Cake 105
Moroccan Rice, Sweet 94
Moussaka, Rice.. 74
Muffins, Ham and Zucchini 15
Muffins, Peach and Pecan.......................... 21
Mulligatawny Soup......................................5
Multigrain Bread.. 12
Mushroom and Sun-Dried Tomato
   Risotto 80

N, O

Nasi Goreng 98
Neapolitan Rice Cake 60
Nicoise Salad, Rice 64
Nut Cake with Coffee Creme
   Anglaise, Double 100
Nutty Cheese and Rice Frittata.....................4
Nutty Olive and Rice Meatloaf 75
Old-Fashioned Creamed Rice 116
Orange Buttermilk Pancakes.................... 117
Oregano Chicken with Cheesy Rice
   Topping.. 50

P

Paella, Chicken and Seafood 33
Paella Croquettes 18
Paella, Quail and Mushroom 71
Pancake, Indian Rice 89
Pancakes, Hazelnut Praline..................... 118
Pancakes with Red Pepper Sauce,
   Salami..9
Parmesan Risotto with Veal and Olive
   Ragout.. 59
Peach and Pecan Muffins........................... 21
Peanut and Sunflower Seed Pilaf 87
Pecan Muffins, Peach and.......................... 21
Pepper and Prosciutto Rice Cake 4
Pepper Halves with Tomato Rice,
   Roasted.. 34
Pepperoni Risotto 28
Pesto, Rice and Vegetable Soup 7
Pesto Risotto with Meatballs...................... 28
Pikelets with Nutty Pepper Salsa,
   Buttermilk... 23
Pilaf, Peanut and Sunflower Seed 87
Pilaf with Crunchy Marinated Chicken,
   Indian... 31
Pizza with Red Pesto, Rice and
   Artichoke.. 26
Plum and Hazelnut Rice Strudel 109
Polenta Stars in Orange Syrup 119
Polenta with Mushroom Cream
   Sauce, Rice.. 52
Pork Biriani 62
Pork Parcels with Rice, Bacon
   and Beans.. 55
Pork Salad, Barbecued 91
Pork Stir-Fry in Rice Baskets, Roast 11
Pork with Fruity Rice 48
Prawn and Chicken Patties 64
Prawn Combination Rice, Chilli
   Crab and.. 71
Prawn Risotto 67
Prosciutto and Rice Frittata, Leek,.............. 22
Prosciutto Rice Cake, Pepper and 4
Prosciutto, Veal Cutlets with Sage
   Rice and... 58
Pudding, Brown Sugar Rice 116
Pudding, Mexican-Style Rice.................... 106
Puffed Rice Crisps with Chilli Relish........... 26
Pumpkin Rice 68

Q, R

Quail and Mushroom Paella 71
Quail with Rice and Apricot
   Seasoning, Roast 50
Red Pepper Rice Pastries, Lamb and 36
Rhubarb and Apple Cobbler 115
Rice and Artichoke Pizza with Red
   Pesto... 26
Rice and Avocado Salad 94
Rice and Barley Country Soup.................... 15
Rice and Cheese Torte.............................. 12
Rice Anise Terrine with Summer Fruits 102
Rice Cake with Crispy Potatoes
   and Dill... 86
Rice Crisps 16
Rice Moussaka 74
Rice Nicoise Salad.................................... 64
Rice Polenta with Mushroom Cream
   Sauce 52
Rich Chocolate Fudge Cake..................... 111
Risotto, Kumara and Fennel 88
Risotto, Mocha.. 106
Risotto, Mushroom and Sun-Dried
   Tomato 80
Risotto, Pepperoni.................................... 28
Risotto, Prawn 67
Risotto with Eggplants, Baked 57
Risotto with Meatballs, Pesto 28
Risotto with Veal and Olive Ragout,
   Parmesan.. 59
Roast Pork Stir-Fry in Rice Baskets 11
Roast Quail with Rice and Apricot
   Seasoning 50
Roasted Eggplant, Pepper and Rice
   Salad 82
Roasted Pepper and Garlic Rice................ 88
Roasted Pepper Halves with
   Tomato Rice.. 34
Roasted Vegetables with Harissa
   Rice Salad.. 61
Rosemary and Parmesan Rice Chips 87

S

Saffron Rice.. 98
Saffron Rice Gumbo with Seafood 75
SALADS
   Asparagus Mushroom Salad with
      Rice Pesto 97
   Barbecued Pork Salad.......................... 91
   Jasmine Rice Salad with Chilli
      Coconut Dressing 90
   Rice and Avocado Salad........................ 94
   Rice Nicoise Salad 64
   Roasted Eggplant, Pepper and Rice
      Salad.. 82
   Roasted Vegetables with Harissa
      Rice Salad.. 61
   Smoked Chicken and Rice Salad 6
   Triple Rice Salad 94
   Warm Lamb and Wild Rice Salad............ 36
Salami Rice Pancakes with Red
   Pepper Sauce 9
Salmon and Rice Fillo Pastries, Thai........... 73
Salmon Rice Patties with Tartare
   Sauce 41
Satay Rice, Spicy 93
Sausage and Pepper Casserole,
   Crunchy-Topped 44
Seafood Paella, Chicken and..................... 33
Seafood Rice Flans, Creamy...................... 72
Seafood, Saffron Rice Gumbo with 75
Seasoned Baked Squid.............................. 67
Seasoned Spatchcocks with Port
   Sauce 42
Shortbread Butterflies, Walnut and
   Rice 103
Smoked Cheese and Rice Pears................ 91
Smoked Chicken and Rice Salad...................6
Smoked Fish and Rice Strudels.................. 47
Smoked Salmon Kedgeree Filling,
   Gougere with.. 49
Souffles, Date and Butterscotch............... 106

SOUPS
   Corn and Coriander Soup 5
   Creamy Chicken Soup with Cheesy
      Rice Balls..6
   Mulligatawny Soup 5
   Pesto, Rice and Vegetable Soup...............7
   Rice and Barley Country Soup 15
   Spicy Minestrone Soup with Rice
      Croutons...6
   Wonton Soup 14
Spanish-Style Rice with Potatoes and
   Onions.. 67
Spatchcocks with Port Sauce,
   Seasoned... 42
Spicy Chicken with Salsa in Rice Cups 20
Spicy Minestrone Soup with Rice
   Croutons...6
Spicy Minted Meatballs.............................. 76
Spicy Patties with Coriander Cream
   Sauce 8
Spicy Prawn and Chicken Patties............... 64
Spicy Satay Rice 93
Spinach Rice 85
Squid, Seasoned Baked 67
Steak and Mushroom Pies......................... 30
Sticky Rice Rolls 10
Stir-Fry in Rice Baskets, Roast Pork 11
Sushi 10
Sweet 'n' Spicy Jamaican Chicken............. 70
Sweet Moroccan Rice 94

T, V

Tacos, Bacon, Bean and Rice..................... 20
Thai Salmon and Rice Fillo Pastries........... 73
Thai-Style Fried Rice 98
Tomato Herb Rice 95
Triple Cheese Tempters............................. 20
Triple Rice Salad 94
Veal and Bacon Rolls 55
Veal and Olive Ragout, Parmesan
   Risotto with 59
Veal and Rice Balls in Tomato Sauce 55
Veal Cutlets with Sage Rice and
   Prosciutto... 58
Veal Pilaf, Fruit and Nut 48
Vegetable Flan, Grilled 16
Vegetable Soup, Pesto, Rice and...................7
Vegetable Stack, Curried Rice
   Patties and.. 60
Vegetables with Harissa Rice Salad,
   Roasted.. 61
Vietnamese Rice Paper Rolls 18

W-Z

Walnut and Rice Shortbread Butterflies 103
Warm Lamb and Wild Rice Salad 36
Wild Rice and Orange Mustard
   Sauce, Duck with.................................. 70
Wild Rice Triangles with Creamed
   Leek Topping... 23
Wild Rice with Broad Beans and
   Red Pepper.. 97
Wonton Soup 14
Zucchini Muffins, Ham and 15

QUICK CONVERSION GUIDE

Wherever you live in the world you can use our recipes with the help of our easy-to-follow conversions for all your cooking needs. These conversions are approximate only. The difference between the exact and approximate conversions of liquid and dry measures amounts to only a teaspoon or two, and will not make any difference to your cooking results.

MEASURING EQUIPMENT

The difference between measuring cups internationally is minimal within 2 or 3 teaspoons' difference. (For the record, 1 Australian metric measuring cup will hold approximately 250ml.) The most accurate way of measuring dry ingredients is to weigh them. When measuring liquids use a clear glass or plastic jug with metric markings.

If you would like the measuring cups and spoons as used in our Test Kitchen, turn to page 128 for details and order coupon. In this book we use metric measuring cups and spoons approved by Standards Australia.

● a graduated set of four cups for measuring dry ingredients; the sizes are marked on the cups.
● a graduated set of four spoons for measuring dry and liquid ingredients; the amounts are marked on the spoons.
● 1 TEASPOON: 5ml.
● 1 TABLESPOON: 20ml.

NOTE: NZ, CANADA, USA AND UK ALL USE 15ml TABLESPOONS.
ALL CUP AND SPOON MEASUREMENTS ARE LEVEL.

DRY MEASURES

METRIC	IMPERIAL
15g	½oz
30g	1oz
60g	2oz
90g	3oz
125g	4oz (¼lb)
155g	5oz
185g	6oz
220g	7oz
250g	8oz (½lb)
280g	9oz
315g	10oz
345g	11oz
375g	12oz (¾lb)
410g	13oz
440g	14oz
470g	15oz
500g	16oz (1lb)
750g	24oz (1½lb)
1kg	32oz (2lb)

LIQUID MEASURES

METRIC	IMPERIAL
30ml	1 fluid oz
60ml	2 fluid oz
100ml	3 fluid oz
125ml	4 fluid oz
150ml	5 fluid oz (¼ pint/1 gill)
190ml	6 fluid oz
250ml	8 fluid oz
300ml	10 fluid oz (½ pint)
500ml	16 fluid oz
600ml	20 fluid oz (1 pint)
1000ml (1 litre)	1¾ pints

WE USE LARGE EGGS
WITH AN AVERAGE
WEIGHT OF 60g

HELPFUL MEASURES

METRIC	IMPERIAL
3mm	⅛in
6mm	¼in
1cm	½in
2cm	¾in
2.5cm	1in
5cm	2in
6cm	2½in
8cm	3in
10cm	4in
13cm	5in
15cm	6in
18cm	7in
20cm	8in
23cm	9in
25cm	10in
28cm	11in
30cm	12in (1ft)

HOW TO MEASURE

When using the graduated metric measuring cups, it is important to shake the dry ingredients loosely into the required cup. Do not tap the cup on the bench, or pack the ingredients into the cup unless otherwise directed. Level top of cup with knife. When using graduated metric measuring spoons, level top of spoon with knife. When measuring liquids in the jug, place jug on flat surface, check for accuracy at eye level.

OVEN TEMPERATURES

These oven temperatures are only a guide; we've given you the lower degree of heat. Always check the manufacturer's manual.

	C° (Celsius)	F° (Fahrenheit)	Gas Mark
Very slow	120	250	1
Slow	150	300	2
Moderately slow	160	325	3
Moderate	180 – 190	350 – 375	4
Moderately hot	200 – 210	400 – 425	5
Hot	220 – 230	450 – 475	6
Very hot	240 – 250	500 – 525	7